CW00427965

The Art of Falling Gracefully

or

My Journey with Parkinson's

by
Veronika M.M. Lees

The Art of Falling Gracefully

This Book is dedicated to
my whole family especially
my long-suffering husband, Mick
as well as all my friends who also suffer with
Parkinson's

All profits from the sale of this book will be
donated to Parkinson's UK

The Art of Falling Gracefully

The Art of Falling Gracefully
or
My Journey with Parkinson's

Introduction

When I first began to write this, the story of 'My Journey with Parkinson's,' it was originally meant to be my ramblings of my experiences. If I was asked a question by one of the many doctors or specialists who look after my many ailments, which are a direct result of my Parkinson's, I could go back over it to find the answer, especially if my memory failed me. It was also to show to my family and friends so that they could understand what it was like for me, on a daily basis, as I walk with Parkinson's.

Then I thought there are more than just me, travelling along this pathway, so I made it more readable, more of a story but still a true story, every word of it.

Recently, it has come to my attention that many sufferers, particularly men, hide away at home as they do not want to be seen in public. Neither will some sufferers go to support groups as they think they will see some terrible sights with sufferers shaking, dribbling, and jabbering incoherently in wheelchairs.

The Art of Falling Gracefully

They already see themselves being just like this in a year or so, which of course is all so much rubbish. They do not believe that we are all walking wounded. Just by looking at most of us you could not tell we had Parkinson's, which is exactly why it is such a dreadful disease.

In a nutshell, Parkinson's robs you of the joy in living; each day when you wake in the morning you don't know how you are going to be or what you can accomplish. Sometimes the effort of getting out of bed is all you can do, other days you can feel so well that you accomplish many of the things you normally would have done prior to your becoming ill.

This is the reason I first published this on Facebook in weekly episodes and I asked my readers to share it around. I thought that if I could just get one person out of his/her house and get on with his/her life it would all have been worthwhile.

Today there are about 127,000 people in the UK suffering with Parkinson's, i.e. 1 person in every 500 and 2 new people are diagnosed with Parkinson's every hour. Parkinson's has over 40 symptoms from tremor and pain, to depression and anxiety. Some symptoms are treatable, but the drugs can have serious side-effects which can range from nausea and vomiting to heart failure and death. There are 127 different types of Parkinson's which makes finding a cure all the more difficult.

At the time of writing this our local Parkinson's nurse in Eastbourne, Becky Mitchener, has about 700 people to look after whereas she is only supposed to have 350. Her area ranges from Newhaven to Bexhill and up as far as Uckfield. Becky currently holds clinics in Seaford, Uckfield, Hampden Park and in the Eastbourne District General Hospital ("DGH"). As far as her patients are concerned, she is an absolute angel and we all love her.

19th May 2020

All profits from the sale of this book will be donated to Parkinson's UK

Table of Contents

Page

Appendices

Prequel

Before I start, I think I should explain that my Father had Parkinson's. He had a shake in one hand. He was diagnosed privately and started on what was probably Sinemet which gave him violent attacks of Dyskinesia. (Dyskinesia is when you have completely uncontrollable involuntary movements either when you are at rest or when you are trying to do something specific such as threading a needle or writing a letter.) Dad could not stay in bed either and whatever time he woke that was when he had to get up.

My Mother suggested he cut the tablets down to just one in the morning and that is what he did. He still suffered with restless legs, but the violent attacks of Dyskinesia eased somewhat, although he still hopped out of bed as soon as he woke up.

My Mother is not comfortable with nursing and was dreading when he became worse. Mum is a person who gets depressed very easily and the thought of my Dad being bed-ridden and possibly doubly incontinent was more than she could have coped with and, more importantly, more than what my Dad could have coped with.

Fortunately, God had other plans and my Dad suffered

a massive heart attack the evening after he had attended Paul's funeral. Paul was Moira's husband and Moira was my Dad's favourite cousin. Dad never recovered consciousness after his heart attack and was taken to intensive care where three separate brain stem tests were carried out. Our Parish Priest was also urgently called and arrived at University College Hospital in West Croydon (formerly Mayday Hospital) to give my Dad the Last Rites. Needless to say, my Dad failed all three tests and we were left with the decision as to when we should turn off the ventilator. My Mum told us all to go to work the next day and she sat with him until he breathed his last..... Dad died just two years into his 'Journey with Parkinsons'. I think it is only now that I realise how lucky he was, as I am now on the verge of completing the sixteenth year of my own journey.

David Major, who is a good friend and fellow Parkinson's sufferer, teaches Tai Chi at the Alice Croft Centre in Eastbourne. I met him there when we both started learning Tai Chi with Graham on a Thursday. For a couple of years whenever Graham was on holiday David and I would take the class. It was David who dreamt up the title of this book. It kinda of grew on me as it hides the horrors of my falling and hurting myself over 130 times in the last three to four years. On average, about once a month, I can be found seated in A&E at the DGH waiting to see a doctor or waiting for a CT Scan after I have banged my head. I do not count when I fall on a bed or soft chair or sofa. If I did the number of falls would be well over 400.

Another close friend, Andrew Lees, who I met with his wife Susan, when giving out literature on Parkinson's in our local Shopping Centre during a Parkinson's Awareness Week ("PAWS") about four or five year ago, volunteered to proof read this small book for me. We had a good laugh when he told me his name and then I told him about my own son, Andrew Lees and his wife who was christened Suzanne. Well after that he calls me Mumsie and I call him My Son and we laugh when people hear us because he is a few years older than me. I am very grateful to him for picking out the last few typos that both I and my husband, Mick, had missed.

A word of warning :- my readers should be aware that some of the later falls in this book are quite dramatically described and all I can say is " Imagine Yourself in My Shoes" and you will feel every bruise and bump that I have felt.

19th May 2020

Chapter 1 – Telling Mother

"I don't know what is wrong with you Mrs. Lees" said the Professor at Mayday Hospital to whom my GP had sent me, "but one thing I can say for certain is you do not have Parkinson's Disease. So, I am going to send you to a higher authority." He was, of course, totally wrong and I really did not believe what he was saying as I was convinced that I did have it. My Dad's variety of Parkinson's was the more common version. One of his hands shook and he put his hand into his trouser pocket to hide it. I understand that this type of Parkinson's is hereditary but mine was just bad luck, or so I have been informed.

For five years my legs had been bounding about as if they belonged to a mad puppeteer who liked to see his puppets dance. Every morning I, like everyone else, paid a visit to the bathroom and to keep me entertained my left foot started very gradually to tap dance. Over a period of several months the right one slowly joined in and gradually over the next few years my feet rebelled so much that I could no longer hide them. They danced wherever and whenever they wished. The only way to stop them was to stand up but my feet still had electricity in them, and my legs shook.

The Art of Falling Gracefully

Events took another year to come to a head. Mick had a minor stroke a couple of weeks or so before Christmas in 2008 and six months before he was due to retire at age 60. He was in hospital for about 10 days and was discharged two days before Christmas just in time to welcome our youngest son's future in-laws to dinner. My husband joined in all the Christmas festivities, but he retired early. After the joys of Christmas were over, Mick went for a walk around the block hanging on to me and a walking stick. What took him 5 minutes before took 45 minutes then, but he persevered and gradually the timing improved. Two weeks later I returned to work and my husband continued to make good progress. By the end of August both of us had retired so we decided to go to Medjugorje, a small village in Bosnia Herzegovina, where Our Blessed Lady still appears to certain visionaries, on pilgrimage in September 2009 to thank Her for his recovery. We took my Mum with us as well as my niece, Dr Clare, who was specialising in palliative care. Whilst we were away, I had a lot of pain in my back and I had developed a rash. My niece diagnosed me with shingles and said I should see my GP, not only to get strong painkillers for the shingles but also to tell him about my dancing legs. I said that I would not have to tell him he would see it for himself.

For my part I believed I had Parkinson's but when the Professor said I hadn't, I phoned my Mum and told her what he had said. I suppose she would have phoned me anyway. It was the first in a long line of big mistakes.......

Eventually I received an appointment to see the top neurologist at Atkinson Morley (now part of St George's hospital, in Tooting) and off we went. The first thing he said to me was "Good Morning Mrs. Lees. You have Parkinson's Disease". I responded with "The Professor at Mayday told me that I definitely had not". I gloss over the pantomime of his "Oh yes you have" and my "Oh no I haven't".
"Well I will have to prove it to you" he eventually said. "You will have a DAT Scan."
"What's that?" said I.

He explained what was going to happen; after which he told me he expected that I had lost about 2/3rds of my dopamine producing cells. He said for good measure I would also have an MRI Scan done on my spine. This would be the first of many MRI Scans done on my back over the next few years.

As we left his office, I did not know what to think. The phone was ringing when we got home. It was my Mum "Well?" she said. I managed to say Parkinson's before she and I dissolved into tears and needed lots of handkerchiefs. Mick took the phone from my hand and explained what was going to happen.

Chapter 2 – Glowing in the Dark

A short while later my appointment for the MRI Scan flopped down onto the mat and a week later I had a phone call from the hospital saying that they would be sending some pills for me to take, both before and after the DAT Scan. They gave me a date to start taking them and also explained that these pills were to protect my thyroid.

The day before the DAT Scan the phone rang again. Would I confirm that I was definitely coming for my appointment? I did not know why they rang me as I always kept doctors' appointments and, like my Dad, was always early. I replied that I was coming.
"OK" the voice said, "We can order the injection."
"Pardon" I said.
The voice continued, "We have to have the injection flown in specially from America. It has a half-life of a week. It's very expensive. Think all together it costs £10,000. See you tomorrow" said the voice and the line went dead.

My brain went into overdrive. I had schoolgirl physics and knew that I had heard of a half-life and that it had something to do with radioactivity. I went on the Internet thirsty for more information and discovered that they were going to inject me with a radioactive isotope and I had to stay away from people, especially the young and the old, for a week afterwards.

My husband phoned the children and explained the next step. The two oldest, Andrew and Debbie, who both lived reasonably close, came round. Our youngest, Adam who lives in Yorkshire joined in through the wonder of Skype and asked in a deadpan voice whether or not I would be glowing in the dark. Needless to say, the mood was lightened, and we laughed. Over the following years we have laughed a lot; so much better than dissolving into a pile of soggy handkerchiefs (though if truth were told a number of soggy hankies did quietly hit the wash bin).

The next day inevitably dawned and we duly arrived at the hospital. I stuck out my arm and was injected. The nurse then told me to go and find a quiet corner in the hospital and sit for two hours so it could all circulate around. Quiet corner, oh give me a break ..... in a hospital!

In the end I found a quiet spot in the staff canteen. They must have been used to outsiders like myself as nobody questioned my right to be there as I sat quietly having a cup of tea as I nervously turned the pages of a magazine.

After the relevant time had elapsed, I made my way back to the scanning department and after a few minutes was laid out in exactly the same way as for my MRI Scan and we were off. I was amazed when they said to me that I could go home as it was as if it had never happened. It didn't hurt at all. I returned home with the admonishment in my ears of "Remember to stay away from the old and the very young for a week." Mick, who must have thought he was old at 60, abandoned me for a week and slept in the guest room!!!

Chapter 3 –A Four-Legged Friend Arrives

While all this had been going on Mick had mentioned on many occasions that he would like to have a dog, but not just any dog. He wanted a big dog, a great big dog, a Dulux sized dog.......

Our house has never been suitable for "a big dog," far too many ornaments and odd antique pieces so I decided to take the bull by the horns when one day I saw an advert for Westie puppies. So with Mick's agreement I rang the number and was told that the last puppy had just gone but that they would be breeding from their dog Daisy and their son's dog Scruffy in the Spring but would we like to go round and meet Daisy and Scruffy, the "soon to be again" happy parents. Mick and I jumped at the chance. This was in the Summer of 2009 just after we were back from our Thanksgiving Pilgrimage.

We arrived at the breeder's house which I was pleased to see was spotless. She told us she had been a professional tailoress for many years and had now converted what was her sewing room into a dog room. She showed it to us and also where Daisy and Scruffy slept. It could not have been cleaner.

On hearing our voices, they both came bounding in

and headed for us both for a cuddle. This I have subsequently discovered is the way with these dogs. If a burglar broke in they would be there, lying down inviting the person or indeed person's unknown to tickle their tummies. After that and seeing how well we got on with the dogs we were offered dog care classes once a fortnight and so we became regular visitors on a Tuesday morning for an hour or so.

Chi-Ing, the breeder, taught us everything from nutrition to teeth cleaning, from bathing to brushing and we joined in. Daisy was so good to us, but her offspring born the following February 2010 was of a different breed. When Daisy had given birth, we were told not to come for two weeks as the babies could be disturbed, and the mother could get very fractious. Two weeks later and we were back. We chose the first born, a female dog which we called Holly. Nathaniel, our grandson, changed it to Holly Dog and that name has somewhat stuck ever since.

Her true character came to the surface once she was home. She refused all teething toys and decided to chew the brand-new cupboard under the sink instead or her little step which let her down gently into the garden room from the kitchen.

Cleaning her teeth was a disaster as she bit the head off every toothbrush we tried on her, even the expensive Wisdom ones.

If you went near her face with a comb or brush, you would get a loud wail and possibly a nip on your fingers for your pleasure.

When Holly Dog came home with us the breeder was insistent on giving us two blankets for her as well as home cooked meals for a fortnight. House training took on a whole new meaning as we quickly discovered that she "peed" everywhere, so I decided we had to restrict her whereabouts to the garden room and two square metres in the kitchen. We covered the floor with paper, but she spent all day tearing it up, so I had a rethink and I got my sewing machine out and sewed old towels together and then stuffed them full of paper. This worked, so I spread them all over the garden room and in the two square metres of space she was allowed in the kitchen. Once she got used to this, we gradually removed a towel a day and it continued to work. She went to have her final check and to have her booster jab and a week later I kicked the last towel out the door and hey presto she got the message and went to the door when she needed to go; except when my Mum came round, then she reverted to type.

She got so excited that she peed herself! And not just a dribble either. She totally emptied her bladder and then danced in it. So only after her
feet and undercarriage had been cleaned to Mick's

satisfaction was she let loose and then, you guessed it, she lay down and wanted, no expected my Mum to tickle her tummy. Gradually her tendency to pee herself calmed down and she was allowed to greet my Mum at the door, but she still went bananas whenever she saw her and ran backwards and forwards like a demented fruit-bat......

Ah the joys of dog ownership; I could write a book on her antics!

But I have digressed enough, except to say that Mick was told after his stroke that he should walk, so getting Holly Dog saved his life because to start with he had to take her for short walks five times a day. Gradually these became longer, and we bought him a special rucksack to carry her in which could take a dog up to 10 kgs. We put her in it and off we went walking to the woods and she could then walk a bit before she went back up. Mick was bothered that she would pee in her bag but when she wanted out, she stood up so Mick relaxed after that.

Chapter 4-Pass Me a Bucket Please

I was back to see the neurologist a week later.
"Well" he said, "I was partly right and partly wrong".
Hope sprung within me to be squashed down immediately as the Doctor went onto say "I was definitely correct in my diagnosis but wrong on the level of loss of dopamine cells. You have lost over 90%" and he invited me to have a look at the DAT Scan.

There were just two small pin pricks of light beaming out of the darkness of my brain, instead of the two fat commas of dopamine producing cells, which is what people without Parkinson's have. He then turned his attention to my MRI Scan and informed me that there was a high level of wear and tear down my spine and asked me if I had been a builder in a previous existence. He also informed me that I, like many others, seek a diagnosis after having had Parkinson's for about five years.

I was prescribed Trihexyphenidyl for my tremors and, as the Professor at Mayday had retired, he referred me back there, at my request, to be under the care of the new lovely lady neurologist. I took my tablets, one in the morning and one in the evening and the tremors stopped. I was normal again; but I wasn't and never would be again!

The next month's tablets which were a mixture of two different brands, made me nauseous and after struggling with sickness I went back to my GP and he telephoned my neurologist at The Mayday who prescribed Domperidone which I took for nine years. More recently it has been discovered that it can cause heart failure or lead to severe cardiac complications. So now I have to have an ECG twice every year to check my heart is OK.

When I eventually came off Domperidone I understood that there had been 85 deaths and 287 severe complications as a result of people taking this drug. I think I became number 288, but more about that later.

Chapter 5– Disaster Strikes!!!

About a year after taking medication I began to ache all over when I did anything, and I was incredibly stiff. My neurologist prescribed Co-careldopa/levodopa under the brand name Sinemet which did the trick and it was about this time that I started to wake up about 2.30 a.m. and could not stay in bed. When your day starts at 2.30 in the morning and finishes at 10 at night you get a lot done. Once again Mick left me and moved to one of the guest rooms. I was averaging about 35 hours sleep a week, if I was lucky. Mick needed about 56 hours.

It was about this time our daughter, Debbie, and her husband, Simon, came to see me and told me that they wanted to have more children but they could not afford to buy a bigger house in the vicinity.

Debbie then told me that they had decided to move to Eastbourne which was an area that they knew very well. Mike and Maggie were friends of Simon's parents and they owned a holiday home in Sovereign Harbour. Debbie and Simon had gone there for many a free holiday, which had been the arrangement they had with the owners, who had given them these Holiday Rites as their wedding present. Mick and I had also been down a couple of times.

Simon then asked if we would like to move there as

well. My heart had originally sunk at the idea that they would be moving so far away, and I was so pleased that Simon had asked us to move with them. We had been looking after our grandson, Nathaniel, four days a week and we had both become very attached to him. He arrived at 7.30 am and we gave him his breakfast, dinner and tea and bathed him and got him ready for bed. Afterwards we would sit at the bottom of the stairs singing songs waiting for Debbie to fetch him home. The thought also crossed my mind that if we didn't move with them, they would have no one to look after him.

I always had a hankering to live by the sea and Mick was very happy about moving there as well. We had a five-bedroom house over three floors which was far too big. We knew we had to move because of my problems but had not decided where to go. When your eldest has moved to Uckfield and the youngest lives in a village near Leeds you are in a bit of a quandary.

That summer we hired a bungalow for a week and spent the whole-time map in hand driving around looking at the different areas working out which we liked, and which were an absolute no-no. On our map we marked in where the supermarkets, libraries, the school and, of course, where the Catholic churches were.

In 2011 both families put their houses on the market and things were going great until Mick complained about chest pains walking home one day. You see in May 2011 I had my 60th birthday and Debbie planned to surprise me with a BBQ with all the children and grandchildren in attendance. We knew that Andrew was bringing his family up from Uckfield, but we were not aware that Adam was bringing his family down from Leeds. We decided we would walk down the hill to Debbie's house so Mick could have a couple of beers. The walk down the hill was fine but the walk back up was a different matter. Mick became very breathless and said his chest was just a little tight. We were nearly home by then, so I told him to sit on the wall and wait while I took the dog home and dumped the bag in the kitchen. By the time I had gotten home and done everything I went out the front door to see Mick walking in.

He said he would see the doctor in the morning. Our GP sent him straight to hospital. He came home, hours later, to say he needed a triple heart bypass. He had to go to Kings College hospital, in London for his operation and as the day dawned, they switched his operation from the afternoon to the morning. (The gentleman whose operation was that afternoon had other complications and, unfortunately, he died the same day after his surgery. May God rest his soul.)

We had postponed the sale of our house and had agreed to write a letter to the agent promising that we would give them the right to sell the house again when

The Art of Falling Gracefully

Mick had sufficiently recovered. By the end of February 2012 Mick was well enough to consider restarting the sale of the house again and within four weeks a lovely young couple with a little girl of 2 years made us an offer we could not refuse.

Over coffee I told them we would earnestly look for a house as our daughter was expecting their second child and it was hoped that we would be in residence before she was born. At this point we discovered that we would not have to push our buyers as they were expecting their second child a couple of weeks or so before Debbie's was due. They also informed us that they wanted to keep their current flat and rent it out which slightly removed the pressure on us.

In the end we found a potentially lovely four bedroomed house in the Ratton area of Eastbourne and we moved in on 6th September about two weeks or so before Nathaniel's little sister, Mia-Joan, was born. Our buyers cut it even finer, as we later heard from our old neighbours. Their number two child was born two days after moving in. We had, as usual, bought a wreck and the builders moved in with us. Both the house and the weed-ridden garden needed a makeover.

Chapter 6 – The Builders Move in

As we didn't know the builders in Eastbourne our daughter recommended a company and the boss paid us a visit. I told him that the first thing that was absolutely desperate to be done was on the first floor and I took him upstairs to the third bedroom. The previous owner had taken the window out and had a large set of French doors installed over the dining room extension, but he had not bothered to install any balustrading to keep people from falling off. The builder asked if I had a particular design in mind, and I explained what I wanted was something very simple but every now and then I wanted this Gothic motif put in. I showed him the drawing I had made a couple of weeks beforehand.

A few days later some ironworkers phoned and asked if they could come round to measure up and talk about it. They said the motif I had chosen was a trifle complicated but could be done as they had someone putting it on a computer so that the correct angles could be generated. I said to him not to lose it as we would be wanting both sets of side gates replaced eventually. He asked me how I wanted it attached to the roof of the extension, so I explained that I wanted scrolls attached to the railings and then attached to the walls of the house.

After several more visits to check his measurements,

the balustrading arrived in pieces and was in situ in a day. Our builder then decked it having previously arranged for the roof to be redone prior to the installation of the ironworks. It looked absolutely beautiful when it was finished.

We then discussed the next job we wanted done and we were then told that by Christmas we could either be clean or warm. We opted for cleanliness. The family bathroom was just an enormous shower with jets hitting you from all angles. We could not use it because it was disgustingly filthy, and I had flatly refused to clean it because I thought I would catch something from the bacteria swimming in it. The Jacuzzi bath, which took up a complete quarter of the master bedroom, was so big that half of a primary school rugby team could have sat in it together, was just as filthy. (We had been going round to our daughter's once a week for a bath in the interim.) We were not currently installed in the master bedroom as we moved in with 180 boxes and a good two-thirds had as yet to be unpacked and were scattered about this room.

Mick and I went off to the tile shop and chose floor and wall tiles and then proceeded to the bathroom showroom for the bath suite.

Our builder suggested sinking the bath as far down into the floor as could be done so I could get in and out for longer. He had been told about my Parkinson's. The guys moved in for about a fortnight and when they took the shower motor thing out they asked if we had ever used it to which I replied I would not have let the dog use that shower as it was so disgusting we just shut the door on it. The plumber told me that we had done a very wise thing because if we had we would have flooded the house and he showed me where various pieces had corroded. Thank God for laziness as just for once I had decided to be lazy. If my memory serves, they finished the last bit early on Christmas Eve morning so we could have a bath or use the power shower that was over the bath. It was absolute bliss.

Early in 2013 the builders came again to see about us being warm. The previous owner had taken down the internal porch wall as he had put a new staircase in and needed a little extra space but in doing so he forgot that the porch was a single brick construction and the cold just seeped in.

While they were installing the bathroom, I had designed in my head exactly what we wanted, and once again I produced my drawing for the boss. His young carpenter rose to the challenge and completed the job in record time hiding the joins with different beadings.

We also had the central heating looked at, a new boiler installed, and additional radiators put in and the others upgraded. We then turned our attention to the garden. I wanted an Orangery but decided to make do with a large black greenhouse instead because of the expense. I had planned to lift the flagstones at the bottom of the garden so that I could have a veggie plot, and we lifted a couple of flagstones to see what was beneath. To our dismay we found that the swimming pool, which our neighbours had told us about, had had been filled in with concrete and rubble so there was no hope of growing stuff there. I had three very large 2 feet 6 inches high raised beds installed measuring 9 feet by 3 feet each. I also got the carpenter to make me four large troughs with trellises behind for my runner beans etc.

This was all completed in time for August 2013 and we then held a family party to celebrate the end of the first year's build. It so happened that the date we chose was on the first Airborne day. Airborne is a free air show which is held annually in Eastbourne over the sea with the spectators sitting on the beach. There were also various stalls giving out information as well as food and drink areas and a funfair for the younger at heart. I had no idea this was on as we had been so busy but we were all on the roof terrace standing on the walls as I was afraid our combined weight would make the ceiling cave in as the Red Arrows flew over our heads, flying so low that you could see into the cockpits. One family member was heard to say, "Only Veronika could have arranged for the Red Arrows to fly

over on her party day." I kept very quiet and pretended
not to hear.

Chapter 7- Exercise and Lifestyle Changes

With both Mick and I on regular medication we found a GP in something of a hurry and I was referred to a Parkinson's nurse specialist who recommended me to have a 6-week course in the gym at the DGH. I had never heard of a Parkinson's nurse specialist before, but it was definitely the start of something new. It led me to meet many interesting people which resulted in me eventually becoming the treasurer of the local Parkinson's group and a few years later forming a choir, but more of that later.

The 6-week gym course was an interesting experience. There were about 10 of us present in the gym with an audience of carers. Some people were very withdrawn and others like me were outgoing despite our many problems. I remember a very nice man called Lawrence Baker, who, as time passed became a good friend. He walked with a stick and had a habit of falling over. Between us we brought chaos to the last gym session with the physio, who was looking after us, putting her head in her hands stating that she had never lost control of any group till now. This was all because Lawrence asked me to dance and we proceeded to waltz (more like a shuffle) around the gym but it was in time to the music being played and we did have rhythm.

Sadly, Lawrence died on Friday 27th August 2019 in

the DGH where he had been suffering from sepsis and pneumonia. May He Rest in Peace. Lawrence was a gentleman in every sense of the word with his cheeky grin. He came to one of my parties in 2017 in a wheelchair as he no longer could walk. He could not speak either and used a computer to speak for him. He was greatly loved by everyone and will be missed by all. We pray for Mary, his wife and the rest of his family. that they find peace and acceptance.

After the gym sessions had finished, we were told we could join a waiting list for Hydrotherapy. I put my name down for it straight away. I waited for over a year but eventually a place was vacated, and they offered it to me. Whilst the 6-week gym course was free you had to pay £12 a month for "hydro "and I still go every week although the price has gone down and up over the years. However, it was there I met another charming fellow, Robert Taylor, who totally changed both my life and Mick's as well. He convinced me to go to the local Parkinson's group in Eastbourne. With great trepidation Mick and I went along. I say with great trepidation because we did not want to see people suffering with Parkinson's who were in wheelchairs etc. We did not want to see me as I would be in the future.. ......

But it wasn't like that at all. (Much later I discovered that when things got that bad you stayed at home or were in a nursing home.)

The Art of Falling Gracefully

Robert must have been looking out for me because he came bounding over and introduced us both to all and sundry. Everyone was very friendly, and I no longer worried about dropping things or spilling my tea. I felt at home straight away.

Chapter 8 – The Builders Return

In 2014 they came back to sort out the master bedroom. Mick and I are great believers in working from the top of a house down just in case one had a plumbing disaster which would ruin whatever one had just completed downstairs......

Now the master bedroom when we purchased the house had been knocked into one huge room. Originally, and prior to the house being rented out for ten years, our new neighbours alleged that the owner lived there with three ladies. At one end of this huge room was a king size waterbed and at the other end this monster of a jacuzzi bath with gold plated taps. There was also a sink. No toilet (which would have been the pits).What happened in this master bedroom can only be imagined but one thing is for certain, as it was witnessed by the neighbours, the bedroom windows were suddenly thrown open and bucket after bucket of water was thrown out. One can only think that the water bed had split somehow but the rumour circulating at the time was that one of the ladies got a bit fed up and stuck a knife in it and this was the cause of the inundation in the front garden.

But I digress...... again.

The house, once this owner decided to rent it out, became the favourite home for those stars of the day who appeared at the Congress theatre, such as Jimmy Tarbuck and Little and Large who no doubt enjoyed the peace and quiet that is to be had in Ratton. So how was it that the house was eventually put on the market? When we came to look at the house, we asked the same question and we were told that the previous owner had to sell one of his portfolio of properties to repay the insurance company. Why? That's easy we were told that in his new property he left the printer on which overheated and set fire to the curtains...

So, the owner had to sell one of his properties to cover the costs of the rebuild.

But again, I have digressed........

I had been pondering what to do with the master bedroom and had decided to carve it up into three rooms, a simple bedroom with two equal sized other rooms, one for a walk-in-wardrobe and the other an en-suite but with a huge shower so if I needed a nurse to help me later on that person would remain dry. I think the builders were with us about two months this time but they adjusted all the double glazed windows and doors so draughts were excluded where the fitting was poor and in the case of one window where daylight could be seen down the sides. Meanwhile Mick was busy decorating the other bedrooms.

Chapter 9 – Mother Moves House

For the last couple of years my Mum had been saying that she could not cope with the perpendicular nature of the front garden and it has to be said that you did take your life in your hands clambering about on it. So, she put her bungalow up for sale and started to look for somewhere else to live. She phoned me to say that she had found a small house with one bedroom and a box room. Downstairs there was one large living room, a good sized kitchen and I think that there was a conservatory but she would have to give up most of her furniture and many of the things she had acquired on her travels with my Dad. I could tell she wasn't happy, but it was all that was available.

Anyway, I went online and found for her two options (best not to give Mum too much choice I thought, or we would never get anywhere). The first option was a ground floor maisonette done in a barn conversion which I knew she would like and the second was a bungalow in bungalow city near Hampden Park. We booked appointments for the next day and I sent Mick off to collect her. I telephoned her to tell her to pack her bag as Mick was coming to fetch her to look at a couple of places in Eastbourne. She told me that her bag was already packed as she knew I did not want her to be unhappy giving up all the things Dad and she had acquired on their travel together. When they arrived, I had dinner waiting for them and I informed her what we had arranged for the next day. The appointment at the maisonette was at 10 o'clock and I think the bungalow was scheduled for 2 p.m.

The maisonette was quite dark inside but had been beautifully kept up by the owner who was moving into the upstairs maisonette as she owned them both. Mum was a bit put off when she was told that there was no Damp Proof Course and as it was a listed building you could not inject anything either into the walls; but I could see that this in itself didn't put her off as she could walk round to us on the flat.

That afternoon we went to see the bungalow and I was surprised when we went inside as it was bigger than her existing bungalow and the garden was flat as well. The lady who previously owned it had extended it so that the old kitchen became the dining room and a new kitchen was built next to this. A small conservatory was added as a breakfast room. As for transport, Mum had just a short walk to the bus stop so she could not have been happier. With Holy Mass in town most days at noon she could easily get there during the week (my Mum went to Holy Mass most days) and we could come and pick her up on a Sunday and take her with us to St. Gregory's where she would see Debbie and Simon and the children. She decided to take a second look at the bungalow before she made an offer, which we arranged for the next day at nine o'clock. She liked it even more and when she was told that there were several other people who wanted to view it she was determined that they were not going to go in and made an immediate offer to the estate agent who promised to cancel all the other viewings.

In no time at all moving day arrived. My two brothers, Nick and Francis with their respective wives Celia and Anne, had helped Mum to pack and Nick and Celia bought Mum down in the car to find us waiting to help get her settled. By 5 o'clock with the removal men gone we took Mum back to ours for a rest whilst I finished off dinner which was ready to go into the oven. Nick and Celia joined us saying that they had put the furniture in the rooms as they thought she would like but left the unpacking of her bits and pieces for another day.

With so much achieved it was agreed that they would go home, and we would take over for a few days. They would be back after having a rest themselves from all the packing up that they had helped her with. Nick promised to bring his gizmo which told them where the electric wires and water pipes were behind the walls when he came down next time so he could hang her pictures up.

Suffice it to say by the end of six weeks, we had accomplished so much that it looked as if she had lived there for twenty years. The only real bit of building work she had done was to have the bathroom carpet taken away and the floor tiled. She then turned her attention to the large back garden and for the first time, employed a man to cut the grass and, at my insistence, someone to wash the windows outside. She dug up part of the grass to make flower beds along the edge of the lawn. She painted the large summerhouse a mixture of aubergine and grey and then painted the garden fence to match. She then started to grow her vegetables in whatever bin or bucket she could find as she had an additional piece of land behind her fence with a small greenhouse in the middle. My Mum always grows too much, and she stuffed so many tomatoes, cucumber and peppers plants in her greenhouse I decided that I wasn't going in there ever. You see I have a very large greenhouse and I had made geranium cuttings for my pots. On turning around, I lost my balance and landed in my geraniums and I know if I fell in hers, I would fall through the side as her greenhouse is only about four feet long and three feet wide. Mine is 10 feet 6 inches square.

I asked her, if she was happy living where she was. She replied, "Yes in so far as I can be happy on my own without your Father. I just don't know how he could go just like that and leave me with all the mess to sort out. I never thought that I would live so long after he had gone." This is a well-known mantra which I am sure many of my similarly placed readers will

The Art of Falling Gracefully

understand.

For myself all my life I have been told how like my Dad I was. I just hope that I don't drop down dead at the age of 72 as I have so much left that I still want to do. My bucket list grows with each passing year but when your body tries to outmatch Parkinson's you are going to get nowhere fast, as the next few years would show me in no uncertain terms.

Chapter 10- What happened to 2015

This was the year before chaos started in all aspects of my life which is probably why it was a quiet year. The metal workers returned to do the side gates with the same motif as that for the balustrading. The gentleman had remembered to keep the computer programme so in what seemed little time the two sets of gates appeared and were quickly installed We were also going to decorate the lounge with me doing the wallpapering but this was when I started falling over with such regularity. So we abandoned that idea and got the name of a wonderful decorator who came and priced it up. We told him that he could not start until we had the new double-glazed windows with bevelled glass (with a bit of colour for good measure added) which were expected in a couple of months.

As usual things did not quite go as planned. The decorator phoned to say he could start our job the following week otherwise we would be in limbo for about a year as he had been offered a very large job elsewhere. We asked about the windows which had not yet come. He explained that he could leave a gap and come back to it on a Saturday when the new windows had been installed.

He was as good as his word. He left an exact size gap and as soon as our flashy windows were installed, he came the following Saturday and finished it off. It looked absolutely wonderful and I was so glad I did not have to do it because I felt so tired and I knew I would never have finished it.

Later that same year Mick bought our little Holly Dog, to the Parkinson's group as part of a presentation done by Canine Concern, which was a local group that supplied care dogs to visit nursing homes. Holly Dog had been doing this for a while at different residential homes and the members of the Eastbourne Group got so fond of her that we were asked to bring her to future meetings.

There is many a tale we could write about Holly Dog's exploits including the day she chased a drone round the hall or when she decided to have a closer look at the horn on an old phonograph. She has bought much laughter to the Eastbourne Branch of Parkinsons UK. She still comes to the socials but now shares the limelight with Pepsi, a young deaf dog who is allowed to share Holly Dog's water bowl and her chicken stick treats.

Robert asked me to join the Committee running the group which I did in 2015. A couple of Committee meetings later I found myself thrust into the role of Treasurer. That was an uphill learning curve. I officially took over on the 1st January 2016.

I also started doing Tai Chi as my balance was poor and

this has helped tremendously. (I still take my stick with me when I go out as I have had 13 falls to date.) But surprisingly, I only struggle to remain upright when we do the breathing exercises at the end of the session. I could then even stand on one leg and kick with the other!

Chapter 11- Death Comes Knocking

It was at the beginning of 2016 that the fun really began. My tablets no longer kept my symptoms under control, so my nurse said I needed help with another tablet called Ropinirole. She told me it would help my other tablets to work better. I gradually added in four pink pills and they did help...... for about 18 months....... then my nurse noticed my hands were beginning to swell so I was taken off the tablets and given patches to wear. Trouble was they would not stay on me. They floated off in the shower, in the bath and in the hydrotherapy pool. How I hated them..........but little did I know how much they hated me as well.

The real problem was due to hit me within six months of starting on patches. It began gradually one Thursday in February 2016 when I woke to find my hands were beginning to swell. The next day we were going to visit some friends and I couldn't get my sandals on going there but had to walk barefoot to the car as my feet were twice the normal size. It never dawned on either Mick or me that it was dangerous.

I woke at four in the morning the following day to find my face was so swollen it could have split open. Mick phoned 111 and then rushed me to the DGH where they pumped me full of antihistamines and steroids, enough to fell a racehorse. As the swelling gradually subsided the doctor on duty told me that if I had left it another two hours the Grim Reaper would have had me, and St Peter would have been dolling out my wings and a harp. He also told me if I had any swelling again, I was to go straight back to the hospital.

Coming off the Ropinirole was not good as I was effectively going back to medication, I had been on two years ago. My neurologist at the DGH noticed that my hands and feet were still swollen albeit just a little and she decided to avoid another trip to A&E, so I added an extra tablet every morning, an antihistamine called Cetirizine which so far has kept me out of A&E.

As my tremors were so bad, she tried Beta Blockers, but these made me so unwell my nurse told me to stop them and we had a long chat about the future. In the interim she put me on Half Sinemet at night-time which was a slow release tablet and helped with the overnight stiffness.

Chapter 12- Deep Brain Stimulation

My nurse suggested at our next meeting three months later that I considered having DBS - Deep Brain Stimulation. God help me I thought that that operation was for much later on, not for someone who had just had her 65th birthday.

The operation involves putting electrodes deep in your brain, wiring you up to a battery implanted in your chest and, when they turn it on, your brain fizzes and your tremoring improves as does your walking. You could have it done at Kings College hospital she said, and you won't have to worry about a general anaesthetic as you are awake throughout. You must be joking of course!!!..... I am terrified of the dentist drill........ let alone having someone drilling two great big holes in my head.

My nurse said to think about it. She also suggested I had a chat with someone who had had the DBS done a couple of years ago. This is when a very lovely person called Lucinda Hepp entered my life. First of all, I was in a daze as I went home and told my husband what the nurse had said. While he made me a cup of tea, I turned on my tablet and, on the off chance, went and googled it on Youtube. To my surprise snippets from the operation were shown as well as turning people on, the before and after if you like. It was a miracle what this operation could achieve. But could I survive the staying awake?

It was at this point I phoned Lucinda and she immediately invited me round for coffee the following day. As she lived 15 minutes walk away, I put on my trainers and wandered around. We sat in her lovely garden and she told me of her experience of "staying awake". She said yes you hear the drill, but you don't feel a thing because of the local anaesthetic and once inside there are no nerve endings so you don't feel anything anyway. She told me that she had to keep counting back from 200 so the doctor doing the operation could tell all was well and to take her mind off what was happening. Once the electrodes were in place the holes were sealed and she invited me to feel the two small bumps, one on either side of her head. A day or so later, this time under a general anaesthetic the wires which had been left trailing were pushed under her skin down the side of her head behind her ear down her neck and into her chest where they were joined to the battery mechanism placed there.

After a couple of days recovery to allow for the swelling to go down they turned her on, albeit at a minimum voltage which was gradually upped until the optimum level had been reached which was of course done by trial and error. After she was discharged, she had and still has to go back regularly for checks. The battery lasts about 5 years or so depending on the power used. The battery is usually replaced under a

The Art of Falling Gracefully

local anaesthetic

I knew I had to have this operation. The "after" was so much better than the "before."

We had another family conference and as a result I told my nurse I would go for it but was there a hospital where they put you to sleep because I know if I had to stay awake I would have a heart attack on the operating table. Fortunately, there was such a hospital.

It was about this time that I started having double vision and this totally changed our way of life. I fell down the stairs with a dreadful clatter and ended up clutching the newel post. Mick shouted where are you and what have you done to yourself this time. I never knew he could move so fast!!! He found me laughing at my stupidity. I told him that I had seen two sets of stairs and I chose the wrong one.

When I fell down a second time, he decided something had to be done and we would get a stairlift installed. Not likely I thought and ruin this beautiful staircase. I wondered if someone could install a domestic lift. I went on the Internet and found a company called STILTZ which had been founded by a German man who lived in Australia. He had patented a lift which he had invented when his wife became disabled. It has no machinery in the loft as it runs from a box of tricks on top of the lift. It was a very short time later that we installed a STILTZ domestic lift which whisks me from the lounge to a spare bedroom. It also takes the hoover up and down, plus the washing, our luggage and even little Holly Dog takes a ride occasionally as she hates climbing the stairs with her little legs. My lift has not only become a great talking point at parties as invariably people don't notice it until I quietly go in behind the glass door and wave goodbye to everyone as I am whisked upstairs. However, in 2018 and 2019 I was in such agony that I could not have gone upstairs without my lift.

My grandchildren were heavily into trains and even laid track in the lift so they could play upstairs and downstairs.

A visit to my optician solved my double vision as I bought new spectacles containing prisms which made my eyes work together again.

Chapter 13 – The Builders Come for the Last Time and Mother is Rushed to Hospital

The last big renovation job took place in 2016 when we ripped out the kitchen, utility and downstairs cloakroom. I knew exactly what I wanted and how to go about designing it as I had done it all before on a much bigger scale in our previous home. But now it was a question of getting a gallon into a two-pint pot and I managed it reasonably well. We chose a creamy coloured unit with pewter handles and then we settled down with the designer. She started by asking me what I wanted in the kitchen. She said most people say a sink, a washing machine, a dishwasher, etc with no thought to cupboard space.

I told her I was not daft and promptly brought out my drawings carefully done to scale on graph paper. She was somewhat taken aback as I went on to explain that I wanted curves on everything as I had Parkinsons and I kept falling over and did not want to fall against any sharp edges. My husband could not see from the drawings I had made what the kitchen would look like despite the fact I had talked about every detail even to the sleeping arrangements for Holly Dog under the freezer where she would benefit from the hot air escaping in the cold weather. We came back a few days later to find the designer had three dimensional pictures which Mick just stared at for a few minutes. It looked exactly as I thought it would even down to the shower attachments behind the Belfast sink which would be Holly Dog's bath and would save our backs from using my unusually low bath when washing her.

We then went to the tile shop where I fell in love with these cream tiles which were Egyptian limestone and come straight from the Pharaoh's quarries. They were very big and very heavy. They had to do a special order for the quantity we required, and they said it would be some weeks before delivery. We chose small tiles for the walls. We gave all the details to the builder and the work eventually began. Because the floor tiles were so heavy, they decided that they had to build a wall under the kitchen floor to support the weight, so they gutted the kitchen and took out the floor. Gradually the kitchen came together but whilst the build was progressing, we had other family problems.

Just before the build started my Mum told me that for a few days her eyesight had not been right, and she kept seeing flashing lights. I got very angry with her and asked her why she had not spoken up when she first had the strange lights flashing. She replied that we had been very busy with sorting the kitchen out. Now as I mentioned before Mum only has sight in one eye, so we immediately took her to the eye unit at the DGH. They thought her retina was coming off again, so we were sent to Brighton hospital where they concurred, and she was operated on two days later.

When she came home my brothers and their wives organised a rota for them to come and look after her with me filling in but the last week of our build when I had to be there all the time we had no one to look after her so she went into Shalom House for respite care. It was run by a friend of Mick's and the care she got was first rate. On arrival Mum was asked what she would like in her sandwich at teatime. She told them that she did not eat bread but Ryvita. Then they asked her what she liked to drink tea or coffee. She then informed them that she mostly drank nettle tea as it kept her blood pressure down. At teatime these wonderful people produced Ryvita and nettle tea.

In the end she stayed ten days and then we brought her home. The surgeon had injected oil and gas into Mum's eye and told her she would be able to see again in 6 weeks and 6 weeks to the day she opened her eyes and she could see again. The gas bubble had not completely dissipated and made her a bit seasick, so she kept quite still for a further week until it had totally dissipated.

A short time later Mum asked Mick to take her back to Shalom House so she could thank everyone wo had been so kind to her. She did not go empty handed either but took some large round Sweetie boxes for all the staff.

The Art of Falling Gracefully

Unfortunately Shalom House had to close and was put up for sale a while back as the owner's wife suffered a tragic accident and they could not spend so much time looking after the residents so a decision was made to sell the property.

Chapter 14- The National Hospital for Neurology and Neurosurgery

My nurse sent all my papers to the National Hospital for Neurology and Neurosurgery ("NHNN") with my neurologist's blessing and within three months we were paying our first visit. I was put under the care of Professor Tom Foltynie who did all the usual tests and then he said "We are quite selective at the National Hospital. We don't do the operation and see if it works. We only do it when we know it will work." The test, to discover whether it would work or not was to increase my medication over six months to the maximum. If I stopped twitching and my walking improved and I stopped shuffling and falling, the DBS would work.

So, I doubled the night-time dose of Half Sinemet, and I managed to increase my daily Sinemet intake from 6 to 10 tablets. I still had 6 more to fit in and with the ever-recurring fear of ending up in A&E, I had to progress these extra tablets with great care.

One thing that I do know is that it is going to work as I hardly tremor anymore and my walking has improved and my turning on the spot is no longer a problem although manoeuvring in a small space is still a hazard and I still freeze.

Time will tell and I continue to thank God for the

support of my husband, my three children and their spouses, my seven, soon to be   eight, grandchildren and my dear Mother who moved to Eastbourne at the age of 86, in 2014, so she could keep an eye on me or is it the other way around!

We await events..............................

****

I thought that I had ended my story here but things progressed and my falls became more frequent from my dithery feet and from freezing that I was told I had to continue to write my story, but please be warned some of my falls are terrible and should have an X rating on them.

Chapter 15– Aches and Pains and Help Arrives

At the November 2016 meeting of the Parkinson group I met a lovely lady, Sarah Hill, who did clinical massage for people with Parkinson's. I signed up more or less as soon as I could. Robert Taylor, who was then the Secretary of the Eastbourne Parkinson's Branch, had been the guinea pig for the group and he recommended it. After just two sessions I felt my legs could move properly and I could stride out and walk rapidly and as a bonus I did not drop so many things. I go to her house and climb some very steep stairs hanging on with both hands. Afterwards I go even slower coming down as my feet are very soft from the massage stuff she uses and are also a bit slippery. She plays some lovely music and I admit I nod off. This is very easy for someone who falls sound asleep having an MRI Scan and has to be woken up by the scanning crew!!!!!!!

I also have been invited for regular gym sessions at the DGH on Saturday mornings. Some funding was received from a charitable trust to pay for 20 people divided into two groups overseen by three staff members. Each group has a mixed capability from those who can scarcely do anything for themselves to those who can still do most things. Those more able have a contest each week to see who cycles the furthest or who walks the quickest on the treadmill. The hour passes very quickly and I for one stagger to the car and then flop into a chair at home for a ten-minute shut eye. Mick asked me if it was worth it and I said I would do anything going to stay reasonably fit. After all, if I didn't, he would have to do everything in the house and the garden! (I did not realize at the time how prophetic that last statement was.)

At our usual November coffee morning where we raise much needed funds, Mavis who runs the jewellery stall, called me over and asked me if I had a cleaner ......I said I hadn't but it was beginning to be a dreadful chore as I lived in fear of falling over. She called a lady over and introduced me to her. However, she was waiting for an operation and would not be able to start for some time. So Mick and I went and bought a cordless Dyson and a steamer to tide me over. Her operation was postponed so Selina, our cleaner, duly arrived one Monday morning and I was amazed at what she did in two hours and, more importantly I realised just how slow I had become.

Chapter 16- We Await Events

This was how I ended the first part of my journey and it didn't take long before I found myself in trouble.....big trouble.

I had decided to increase my tablets two at a time at the end of each month so I should be on 16 Sinemet tablets by the beginning of May. A simple strategy you would think giving my body time to settle between doses. It never happened. I upped my tablets to 12 and landed myself in trouble. My balance went off and coupled with freezing I had five falls in two weeks, two of them in one day. To date I have had twenty-eight falls with only the last having a soft landing as I landed on my bed.

My most spectacular fall was the eighteenth one which saw my butt coming into contact with a small brick pillar, three rows high. God but that hurt.....I screamed as I landed and little Holly Dog shot out of the back door closely followed by her Master to find me crying in pain. It was a while before I managed to get up and as I staggered inside, I discovered the imprint of the pillar on my butt showing the bricks and the cement. The bruises took days to arrive and weeks to die down. I still had some slight bruising some two months later. Sitting down was another matter. I needed three soft bed pillows to sit on and I went around the house carrying them from room to room chanting to myself:-

IN EVERY WAY
AND EVERY DAY
IT GETS A LITTLE BIT BETTER

This was the same chant that the new mothers used to say in the East Surrey Hospital's Maternity Ward in Redhill where our first two children were born, when they moved about the ward after having had their babies and, following an episiotomy, had to be stitched up.

I also developed peak flow Dyskinesia as well as facial Dyskinesia. I found it very difficult sometimes to speak. Mick said I didn't sound any different, but I knew there was a problem. I reported back to my Professor and he prescribed Amantadine. Within an hour of taking my first tablet I developed full blown cystitis-like symptoms and an hour later became incontinent. Fortunately, I was sitting down in the garden potting up something or other. Just as well I stay at home when taking new meds.....

My head felt like it wasn't mine and I was away with the fairies most of the time. For example, when counting the money from the next Parkinson's social I kept looking at a coin and I could not make out what it was. I thought it was a foreign coin. It was, actually, a twenty pence piece. Nine days later I took myself off the new tablets as I could not swallow anything, and would, most probably, have starved myself to death albeit over a longer period than most would have taken.

Professor Tom and I had a long chat on the phone, and he told me there was no other medication as good as Amantadine that could help me so I would be put forward for the DBS. My faithful followers will remember the DBS. It's where they drill two ruddy great holes in your head, pass down two wires deep inside your brain and wire you up to a battery pack in your chest. Yes, I know you know the rest, but some readers may not. They switch you on and your brain fizzes and hopefully you can walk much better and the falling over is diminished. Whenever I think about the DBS I think about that film "Carry on Screaming" about Frankenstein and his inventor played by Kenneth Williams saying "Frying tonight" as he rose out of the batter tray.

Professor Tom would be organising three appointments for me for:-

a) an MRI Scan,
b) Psychoanalysis, and
c) the Levodopa Challenge

The Art of Falling Gracefully

I would have the surgery in five or six months, and I should be all healed up by Christmas 2017.

With the departure of the builders we were basically left with the hall, stairs and landing to paint but I had a hankering for the floor to be tiled and what's more, after seeing many tessellated floors in Italy on a tour we had done before I went downhill so much, I wanted one as well. I kept very quiet and scoured the Internet eventually finding some large tiles with small tiles stuck on them which made them look tessellated. They also had some special tiles with a pattern on them to make one motif in the centre of them all. They were in a warehouse somewhere in South Wales, so I got some samples and showed Mick and I explained what I wanted to do. As many of my friends either visited with sticks, walkers, or in wheelchairs, he agreed. We measured up and ordered them and the tiler came and put them down. They looked wonderful and so our house was finished.

Chapter 17- The MRI Scan

A very short while later an envelope from the hospital dropped onto the mat giving details of the where and when I was to go for the MRI Scan. It was to be on a Sunday but not just any old Sunday it was the 28th May 2017. This was a special day in the calendar as I had organised my Mum's 89th birthday party for that day. Wanting to be seen to be proactive I told my Mum that I had to go to town on 28th. For weeks after all I got was "Such a shame you missed my party" but never mind Mum there is always next year!

My husband, typically, went to the station and organised cheap tickets and off we went. We arrived in plenty of time and as they had had a cancellation I was in and out before I knew it, as once again, yes I know..........I fell asleep in the scanner.

We then began the wait for the second appointment. When July came and still nothing slammed down on my doorstep, I telephoned Professor Tom's secretary but was informed that I had to contact the co-ordinator of the DBS team. Nobody had said anything to me about a different phone number. The co-ordinator was very helpful and the lady in charge there had just started two weeks holiday. Two weeks later I telephoned again to be told I should have a letter by the end of the week. True to her word the letter dropped through my letter box the following Saturday informing me that the three tests would be done on the 13th and 14th September. The letter stressed I had to have an escort so once again my husband visited the station to see what cheap tickets were available.

Meanwhile my appointment with my lovely Parkinson's nurse was creeping ever closer so I thought I had better organise my annual ECG to check if the Domperidone had affected my heart or not and thus began another chapter of hospital visits.

Chapter 18- My ECG

For those of my readers who have never had an ECG it's a totally painless procedure. They wire you up, turn a machine on, you wait a minute and they turn it off and take the wires away. The little sticky pads they attach to the wires, however, are a different matter......

Whilst they leave you to adjust your clothing the nurse specialist shows your ECG to your GP. The nurse came back and said, "You have absolutely nothing to worry about". I went home and told my husband it was fine. Two days later the phone rang, and I was asked to make an appointment to see my GP. It wasn't urgent but she wanted to go through my medication. A week later I was sitting in her office and she delivered the bad news. She showed me my ECG and then compared it to the one taken the previous year. The best way I can describe the difference was that instead of being in sinus rhythm with my heart going "boom tiddy" it was going "boom tiddy, tiddy, tiddy."

She said she was going to refer me to cardiology, and they would definitely want me to stop taking the Domperidone. She also informed me that the irregular heart beat could cause clots to ping off and if one got to my brain I could have a stroke so she put me on blood thinners telling me if I had a fall and banged my head or torso I was to go straight to A&E as I could bleed to death internally. They had the antidote at the hospital which is why I had to go immediately.

Most people who have to go on blood thinners are put on Warfarin for which there is no antidote. In my case, however, as I was most likely to have the DBS done in the near future, I was put on Dabigatran Etexilate under the brand name Pradaxa.

Back at home, I decided to have a chat with my nurse so I left a message and a couple of hours later she said she would come round the following Tuesday afternoon. We decided on a plan of action as my suggestion of going cold turkey was dismissed out of hand. I would drop the Domperidone by half a tablet at lunch time, then two weeks later by half in the morning etc. This was ok till day three when I started to feel dreadfully nauseous. The problem was that the underlying medication, Trihexyphenidyl, makes me dreadfully sick which is why I was on the Domperidone in the first place, so I decided that there was no alternative but to go down Plan B as Plan A wasn't working.

Plan B was to come off the Trihexyphenidyl gradually matching the decrease in the Domperidone and see if it worked. No nausea or vomiting occurred. Of course, my tremors returned with a vengeance. But as if by magic the more of the horror drug I dropped the more lucid I became in my thinking and I realised how stifled my thinking had become. I saw the cardiologist the week before I went to London. I had a 24-hour ECG and an echocardiogram the next day. The upshot of the visit was to be discharged back to the GP with the cardiologist wanting me to be on blood thinners for life as they had diagnosed an atrial fibrillation.

Chapter 19 - Hopes for an Easy Solution

With hope with us, Mick and I once again caught the train to London. I had received a two-day schedule detailing an MRI Scan for the first morning, the Psychoanalysis in the afternoon and the Levodopa Challenge the next day.

We arrived at the hospital and were given our station where we would spend the rest of the day. I had thought that Mick could beetle off to the hotel and empty the small suitcases so I could have an early night but we waited and we waited and we waited some more to see where we were going to stay. The nurse came with my file and apologised that I had been kept waiting for my MRI Scan but as I had one in May it was not necessary for me to have another.

We asked her where we were staying, and she looked just a little furtive and said she did not know but the lady at reception could help. Mick went to make enquiries to be told that the lady who should have booked us in to a hotel had her job description changed and they were trying to find us a room.

Lunch came and went, and I was taken for a two-and-a-half-hour session with the psychiatrist. We started with simple things such as I had done in an IQ test for the 11+ examination. But the questions became progressively more difficult. After two and a half hours

The Art of Falling Gracefully

I was totally done in and could not work out simple arithmetic. Since I had been diagnosed, concentration had become a real issue and I could only focus for about 10 minutes. One of his questions was so ridiculous that I told him it was stupid and my reasons why I felt it was so. He did pay me the compliment of telling me he had enjoyed our session and that I was the most cognitively intact person he had seen in his current role.

We returned to our station to be told that they had been unsuccessful in finding us a room and we would have to spend the night in a side room in the psychiatric ward!!! I was lucky I got a bed. My hubby had a mattress on the floor...... It was a far cry from what was in the letter they had sent saying they had booked a hotel room for us. We escaped to the local pub for dinner and retired upon our return hoping for some rest and a decent amount of sleep......

No such luck!!! It transpired that the ward's air conditioning unit was in the en-suite and the fan went on all night. By 5 am my medication was running out and my feet could not keep still so I had a shower and washed my hair......We hadn't bought my hairdryer with us as we were going into a hotel and do you think such items can be obtained in a hospital-of course not!!

The Art of Falling Gracefully

We went into breakfast and I fell flat on my face – fortunately on a large sofa. So, I arrived back at the station in a wheelchair ready for the next instalment. Remember I was to face the Levodopa Challenge which meant no Parkinson's medication after 10 p.m. the previous evening. I was first asked if I would participate in a speech check where I discovered my voice was beginning to tail off at the end of each sentence and I was told to practice SHOUTING..................

I was then taken for the physical testing which proved I was totally unco-ordinated on the left side with useless finger flapping etc etc. Walking was a nightmare as I shuffled and fell in turn. Everything was videoed for posterity to be used as a teaching aid for the students who were interested in Parkinson's.

I was then given 100 mg of Dispersible Madopar which was supposed to work instantaneously but suffice it to say it didn't work as it should have done and one and a half hours later we were still waiting for me to go "On"!!! Once I was "On" everything had to be repeated that I had done when I was "Off."

Eventually we were allowed to leave and arrived home at 10.15 p.m. where I collapsed into bed. I had spoken with my Mum who had been looking after Holly Dog for us and Mick arranged to pick her up the following morning.

Chapter 20 – DBS or no DBS that is the question

A letter came flopping down on the doorstep inviting me to meet the DBS team so once again Mick visited the station and came home with some cheap tickets. This time the appointment was in the afternoon and some dear friends of ours, Ann and David White, came to look after Holly Dog for us. With lunch cooking in the oven for them we were dropped at the station. By this time, I had gotten up to 800 mg of Sinemet during the day (it was easy now I wasn't on the Trihexyphenidyl) and 200 mg of slow release Sinemet by night.

The surgeon came to get us from the waiting room and there seemed to be a lot of people in the room. My consultant, the anaesthetist, a couple of nurses and three or maybe four students. The results of my tests were discussed. We all agreed my tremors had stopped totally with the medication, but the Dyskinesia and Dystonia had to be addressed. (Dystonia is uncontrollable muscle cramps and spasms which are when your toes curl up under your foot). I was asked to show off my walking prowess without my stick. Once I had got going it was fine, but when I was told to stop and turn around, the fun began as the surgeon had to race up the corridor to catch me as my body took off but my feet were frozen to the floor. Good game, I thought; but at least the students learnt what freezing was all about. We went back into the room and I sat down.

The surgeon and my consultant then talked in medical terms which basically I didn't totally understand, but did catch "no to the DBS" as they thought it wasn't necessary but maybe I should be wired up to the GPI (the Globus Pallidus Interna- The motor symptoms of both Parkinson's disease and focal dystonia arise from dysfunction of the basal ganglia, and are improved by deep brain stimulation of the Globus Pallidusl interna) but we would wait and see. And so it transpired. I was asked about my medication and repeated the sorry tale. I was told I had to give amantadine another go but this time in a syrup form.

Promising to ring him if I had the same trouble as before he wrote me a prescription saying it was possible, they hadn't got it in the pharmacy as it was difficult to get hold of. The pharmacy sent us to UCLH to get the only two bottles left which they had set aside for me. (We have no trouble getting it in Eastbourne) Boots were concerned when I said they may have difficulty, but we had none. At one stage I had accumulated 13 bottles of the stuff. We left for the tube and arrived back at Victoria Station with just enough time to have some dinner before setting off home.

The Art of Falling Gracefully

We went back again on 23rd February 2018. Since the last visit I have had seven more falls some bad and some not so. Three times I have managed to land softly on beds, once I fell backwards smashing my left shoulder onto a corner of a concrete pillar in my study, then turning around with phone in hand I fell flat putting out my right knee and left arm. I couldn't kneel on my knee for a couple of months. Then I was getting up from cleaning some windows and my balance just went and I landed half in Holly Dog's basket and half in a large leather armchair. But my final fall was quite spectacular.

Hailsham group had challenged Eastbourne group to a tenpin bowling match. I was halfway through the first frame when it happened. Ball in hand I turned around and my top half carried on, but my feet remained stuck to the floor. I shot the ball from my hand and I went down clobbering my left knee and my elbows and arms. Everyone cheered as I got up and after that every time I sent a ball down they cheered and clapped me on. The bruises took days to arrive and weeks to go.

Chapter 21 – Further Trials

For some time I had felt that my legs would go through my hips and basically I would end up with just my feet sticking out from my bottom, Well I began to have a general ache in the top of them which then developed into real pain. Gradually it went to my back and it became so bad I consulted with my GP. I told her that it was particularly bad when I got out of a chair after sitting for about half an hour. I had to rely on my stick and had to bend right over with every step taken in agony. Only very gradually could I right myself.

She ordered blood tests and an overnight letter went for a hip X-ray and an urgent MRI Scan as I was due in London two weeks later. I was told to visit with her the following week for the results. My blood test results showed that I had an inflammation somewhere and that possibly my thyroid was not working properly. I had to repeat the tests again a week later and the same result came back. I repeated them a third time a month later and the results were unchanged, but my pain was increasing all the time. A couple of weeks later I was called to see the G.P. She told me that my antinuclear antibody test (part of the first set of blood tests), which takes about 6 weeks to come back was positive and the GP thought that I could have rheumatoid arthritis.

The Art of Falling Gracefully

I was booked to see a rheumatologist only to discover on returning from a fortnight in Dorset, that the wait was 45 weeks. I phoned up the appointments people and said that I could not wait that long as the pain was so bad it was affecting my Parkinson's. She asked me to wait for a couple of minutes and when she returned, she told me there was a waiting time of just 15 weeks at three other hospitals. Mick and I chose the Queen Victoria Hospital in East Grinstead. A week or so later a letter came telling me an appointment had been made for me on the 7th August some 8 weeks away or so...... I thought I could manage that especially as my GP had increased my co-codamol to two 30/500 mg tablets 4 times a day. To help with the pain I started taking cannabis oil which I bought from Holland & Barratt.

Later on, in June I saw Becky for my general appointment. I was having a bad day that day, away with the fairies mostly and my speech was bad. I could not even remember all my medications. Anyway, her letter to my GP was quite telling because she copied in the rheumatologist at Queen Victoria who promptly bought forward my appointment to the 10th July.

My falls had risen to 46 by this point with the 45th one landing me in A&E. My dear friend Mary had come round, and I was seeing her out the front door when she saw a cat coming towards me. "Didn't know that you had a cat" she said. At this point, Holly Dog, who loathes and despises cats, shot out the door with me in hot pursuit as I could hear a van coming and all the gardens are all open plan where we live. I was terrified that Holly Dog would be run over. Things went well until I reached the concrete road when, you guessed it, my feet froze, and I fell headlong in front of the van which fortunately had seen Holly Dog and was stopping. I landed on my two front teeth and my right arm and hand took the rest of the fall. Thought I had broken my hand but three X-rays later and my face checked to see if I had broken my jaw or my nose (remember I am on blood thinners) I left A&E all intact but for my teeth, which my nice dentist fixed a week later.

My 46th fall, whilst it did not involve A&E, was nearly as spectacular. It involved a hose pipe and some spare chairs which my husband had carefully stacked so I had a small gap of about 8 inches to go through.... I landed on the pile of chairs as they were collapsing, and my bruises were very spectacular being every shade under the sun. Needless to say, the air was also blue as well....

Chapter 22- The Queen Victoria Hospital – East Grinstead

Mick and I set off with what we thought was plenty of time to spare but we ended up having trouble parking. Eventually we put the car in a nearby side road and I staggered back to the hospital with a stick with Mick helping me. The pain in my back was excruciating after sitting in the car for an hour. We found our way to the out-patients dept and only waited 5 minutes before I was called in. The doctor I saw was interested in rheumatology but was not the consultant. My appointment showed me as being a returning patient and the slot was for just 10 minutes. When the doctor opened my file, she was quite horrified that it just contained my referral letters from my GP and that of Becky, my Parkinson's nurse.

She took 25 minutes to take my history and to examine me. At the end she said she thought I definitely had an autoimmune disease, but it was too early to say which one. She put me on Tramadol for the pain and sent me to have more blood tests and to come back four weeks later.

The staff showed me where the blood tests would be done and then escorted me to the pharmacy for the Tramadol. I have to say they were all very nice and helpful. They gave me back the original appointment on 7th August to see Dr. Makadsi, the rheumatologist who was charming and after examination he thought that I had chronic inflammatory arthritis probably part of Undifferentiated Connective Tissue Disorder. So he put me on Prednisolone (steroids) for six weeks and Hydroxychloroquine 200 mg twice a day.

I started the new regime the following day and by the time two days had gone by I was virtually pain free but the new medication affected my Parkinsons and each evening I suffered with tremors, Dyskinesia and Dystonia in my feet. I reported this back but was told it was not bought upon me by the new medication. To control them at night-time I had to take odd doses of Trihexyphenidyl. Some days I need two tablets and some days only one at night. Gradually these horrors have receded, but I now find I do not sleep very well again. I did stop the cannabis oil for a few days but decided to return to it to see if it helped me to sleep again. According to the letter he wrote to my GP my anti-nuclear antibody test ANA was strongly positive with a titre of 1/2560.

He sent me for more blood tests to check my rheumatoid factor and my ANTI-CCP. Anti-cyclic citrullinated peptide (anti-CCP) is an antibody present in most rheumatoid arthritis patients. Levels of anti-CCP can be detected in a patient through a simple blood test. A positive anti-CCP test result can be used in conjunction with other blood tests, imaging tests, and/or physical examination findings to diagnose rheumatoid arthritis.

Prior to the discovery and testing of anti-CCP, most doctors used rheumatoid factor (RF) – another antibody – as a test to help reach a rheumatoid arthritis diagnosis. I was due to see him again in three months in November. Before then we are back up to London to see Professor Tom at the NHNN in October.

My falls have now risen to 50. My 50th fall was in the house when I fell on Oleg, my little statue of a baby meerkat. God that hurt as it was on the same place as one of the previous falls; so now my bruises had their own bruises. It was the size of an outstretched hand. It took about three weeks to go away.

Chapter 23- London and the NHNN

Prior to my trip to see Professor Tom at the NHNN my falls increased further to 55. It is strange that I have only twice fallen outside of my home environs and that was indoors at the bowling alley and then again indoors at the monthly quiz we attend at the University of Brighton. My fall at the quiz was fairly comical as I do not believe that people had realised that I had Parkinson's.

My team decided that we had been put far too close to two other teams so the decision was made that we would shunt the tables up. The trouble was they shunted it before I had got my balance so down I went. Everyone tried to help me up, but I firmly believe that if you cannot get up on your own you need to go to A&E by ambulance. Mick brought me a chair so I could use it to get up. The rest of the team looked a bit sheepish, but I told them not to worry as I spent quite a bit of time on the floor.

The steroids Prednisolone was gradually reduced to nil after six weeks and the seventh week I remained pain free. The eighth week I became aware of a slight ache in my hips and the top of my legs. This gradually increased until I was in agony once more. On arrival at the NHNN I was staggering along with my stick and my tremors were quite abominable. Professor Tom could not understand why I was in such pain. Fortunately, I had brought with me copies of the correspondence from the rheumatologist which I passed to him. I told him that I had asked him to send copies but obviously this had not happened. I also told him about the hydroxychloroquine and how my tremors returned with a vengeance and my request for different medication.

Professor Tom decided, as an experiment, to up my Sinemet over the maximum of 8 Sinemet Plus to 9.5 tablets a day, adding in a half a tablet three times a day. It stopped my tremors 95% but did nothing for my being rooted to the spot. I had come off the cannabis oil for a few days so I could gauge the effect of the extra pills. On going back on the Cannabis oil, I discovered it did the trick and my freezing improved but did not completely take it away. On reporting back to Professor Tom via his secretary I asked if the medical cannabis would take it away completely and was it possible to give it a try once it was legal.

Two weeks later I was back to square one with regard to tremor and freezing.

Chapter 24- My Hero at the Queen Victoria Hospital

Dr Makadsi, my rheumatologist, listened very carefully when I explained what was happening to my tremors, but he did not know of anyone in the UK being so affected. However, he did reduce the tablets to one instead of two. He also thought that my active autoimmune driven inflammatory arthritis was ongoing, so I was given another short course of steroids. I was introduced to Methotrexate which is a chemo-therapy drug used in treating cancer, but he said it was very effective at very low doses for inflammatory arthritis. I had to take 20 mg once a week. So, I chose a Wednesday and 8 small tablets were added to my Wednesday box. These pills are usually dispensed in 2.5 mg pills.

He gave me a booklet to read which explained all about it including that I had to take folic acid three days after taking the methotrexate to combat any side effects. So, one 10 mg Folic Acid featured in the Saturday box as I had to take them three days afterwards. I also had to have regular eye tests as it could affect my eyesight. I also had to have blood tests every fortnight for the next three months and then every two months, to make sure my liver and kidneys had not been affected by this new drug.

The Art of Falling Gracefully

So far so good and the pain went away. I am still on this drug and the regular blood tests which I have done after Mondays hydrotherapy session show that my liver and kidneys are bearing up well under the onslaught of the Methotrexate.

I booked a six-monthly eye test only to find that my usual optician, who knew about the effects of Parkinson's, had retired but his daughter had taken his place. She said my eyes were fine, but I did have the beginnings of cataracts in both of them.

Chapter 25- A New Hobby

While I was having fun with my rheumatologist, my Parkinson's nurse noticed on one of my regular visits that my voice was disappearing, so I was sent for speech therapy. To my horror I was told my voice level was down to 50 decibels. I had been accusing my husband of going deaf when he ignored what I was telling him. He had been conned by me into going for a hearing test which showed he was slightly deaf in the upper registers but otherwise he was fine. Mick asked the doctor for an example of an upper register sound, he was told it could include the female voice, so he concluded that it was nothing to worry about.....

One of the speech therapists came to my house and started the ball rolling. I had to say "Ah" as loud and as long as I could. After just three "Ahs'" out of ten, Holly Dog retired from the room and went in search of her master who appeared with her lead to say he was just taking the dog for her usual walkies. The fact that she had just returned from her normal "Walkies" was not lost on me. After ten Ah's I had to do 10 "Ahs'" up a scale and then 10 "Ahs'" down the scale for good measure. The Speech Therapist did all this holding a decibel reader in front of me. She then asked me to read a passage from a book. She went away to return the following week to repeat the "Ahs'" etc. Meanwhile she said I had to practice them every day.

The Art of Falling Gracefully

As Holly Dog proved herself to be such a wimp, each morning I went into the shower and practised them with the shower on full blast.

Anyway, after several weeks of working at it I got back to my original loud voice but when I was tired it fell down again. My speech therapist asked me after our last session together if I would like quarterly refresher courses and it was at these classes, I further discovered the scale of speech loss to Parkinson's as the room was full of my friends.

For some reason this bothered me a lot; so I had a word at our next Committee Meeting and they agreed in principal to the formation of a singing group, but any singing activity would have to eventually break even and not be a drain on the group's finances. No one knew better than me the state of the finances as I was the Treasurer. I knew that there was plenty of money in the kitty, but I also could see the hydro unit requiring some cash in the future as the numbers from Hailsham were dwindling. With each departure our costs rose.

The upshot of this was after chatting with various people, we set up a singing group with Nicky Young who had been a professional singer since the age of 16. Her Father, Ron MacGregor, also has Parkinson's and I met Nicky through him as he comes to hydrotherapy. We met once a week at my house until the numbers became too many that we decamped to my church's hall. With the permission of our lovely Parish Priest Fr. Raglan, we pay by donation only for the use of the church hall and one of the group each week rattles our little box until everyone has coughed up a pound each every time we go there. As new members arrive so the donation will go up to a maximum of £16 per hour.

We also have to vacate the premises every second Wednesday each month so I had a rare light bulb moment and as a result we now sing in various Nursing /Retirement homes, I sprung this on them and said next week we are not here we will be singing at a retirement home for the residents. This has resulted in, not only earning some money for the group, but also in improving our reputation and making us all aware of the importance singing brings to the lives of Parkinson's sufferers. We are always fully booked for several months ahead.

Chapter 26- My Parkinson Nurse has an idea

As I was continuing to freeze and fall over with monotonous regularity, Becky my Parkinson's nurse suggested I tried Opicapone and with the Professor Tom's permission we did. Opicapone was supposed to concentrate the dopamine in one place in the brain rather than let it wander all over it.

There was one small snag. I threw up on day three, so it had to be stopped. The neurologist at the DGH suggested we try again but using an emetic as well, so I gave it a go. For three days beforehand I took anti-sickness pills and through the first day as well. I threw up on day two this time. So we abandoned that idea........

When I had been in London last, Professor Tom had mentioned the apomorphine challenge so Becky got Professor Tom's permission to do it at the DGH rather than my going up to London which, as it turned out, was just as well.

In order to conduct the apomorphine challenge I had to be totally medication free. I was in for a big shock when I came off all my medication as I could no longer stand up. My balance had completely disappeared so without all those small yellow Sinemet tablets I would have been in a wheelchair, quite helpless. Becky helped me to stand upright and I walked a few steps but, when asked to turn round, I could not move at all, so she had to dance me back to my wheelchair. Dancing works sometimes where counting one two, one two or left right, left right doesn't. Anyway, we completed all the tests and I scored 43 which is quite bad. She said this would go down as the challenge progressed until the optimum for me was reached. She showed me how to load the ap-go pen and she did the first injection so I would know what it felt like when I did the next. She then said she would be back in five minutes as another of her patients was in hospital and she wanted to check on her.

"That's OK." I said. But just two minutes later I began to feel very peculiar and asked the nurse for a bucket. I knew what was going to happen and I heard the nurse racing after Becky saying I was throwing up. So that was the end of that. Mick was sent for and once I was fairly stable back on my drugs, he took me home. The apomorphine was supposed to stop me freezing and falling over and I had been so hoping it would work as my falls had risen to 67.

Becky wrote to Professor Tom to suggest that the only thing left for me was the DBS.

Chapter 27- Other Matters

At the beginning of March 2019, I awaited my clinic date with my rheumatologist on the 12 March with some trepidation. You see I now have such severe sciatica, or so my GP told me, that I am on Morphine Patches as well as Dihydrocodeine and Diazepam. This all started three days after a simple fall onto my left leg last November 2018. Most days I cannot put any weight on my left foot without screaming in pain. A &E said I should have a second MRI Scan done on my spine; however, the Clinical Community Group or "CCG" have banned GPs from ordering any new MRI Scans. The only way to get one was to be referred to a specialist which, with a waiting time of 33 weeks, was an absolute no-no. My husband arranged for me to go privately and we were seen by a lovely consultant from The Horder Centre in Crowborough, who immediately ordered a full MRI Scan of my whole spine as well as an MRI Scan of my hips.

It is very difficult to remain completely still when your leg is in absolute agony and with a couple of halts, they managed to get my spine scanned. Now when it was the turn of my hips, they wanted me to have this heavy board all over me so my hips could be seen more clearly. In more usual cases I expect it worked but the pain, when they laid it on me, exploded and I admit I screamed somewhat before they took it off.

Easter came and went and the consultant from Horder phoned to give me the results. My hips had some osteoarthritis in them, which was old news to me, but I had early disc degeneration all over my spine But more to the point I had a degenerative Spondylolisthesis at L4/L5 which shows quite marked central canal stenosis with stenosis of both lateral recesses (which basically meant that my Lumbar 4 vertebra had slipped on my Lumbar 5 near the bottom of my spine and my spinal cord was being pinched) and this was the reason why I was in such pain.

At Mick's insistence we were referred to the pain clinic at Horder and I saw a doctor there who said he would shoot an epidural full of steroids into my back at the point the nerves were pinched this, also coupled, with an increase in Gabapentin, which a doctor in A&E had prescribed, on my fourth visit, about the pain in my leg, should sort out the pain. I received a linear steroid epidural from the doctor on the 16th May and there was an immediate improvement in my pain levels. My Gabapentin was ratcheted up from a holding dose of 100 mg three times a day to 300 mg in the morning, 100 mg at early afternoon and 600 mg in the evening.

This worked for a time, but I could feel the pain bubbling and one day I said to Mick that the pain was back. So back we returned to A&E for the fifth time. I saw a recently qualified young doctor who listened very carefully and ratcheted up the Gabapentin still further by 300 mg three times a day (after consultation with a senior doctor). This was only for a week until I saw Dr. Tom Smith at The Horder Centre.

Not surprisingly the increase in Gabapentin affected my balance and the festination in my legs increased so much so that I kept falling over more readily than before.

The doctor was amazed that his strategy had not totally worked but, when you look back on all the different medications, they have tried on me, I was not surprised. The doctor agreed to repeat the injection but also do a nerve block on the left side. The earliest he could do it was in August as he was away on holiday in June and his book for July was full. This gap was alright as we could then go back and have it done at Horder on the NHS.

Chapter 28- Back to London and the NHNN

The day after the injection I was due to see Professor Tom at the NHNN. I was using a walker by this time as my rheumatologist did not like me falling over and lectured me about it whenever I saw him. So my husband ordered patient transport which duly arrived and off we went. Someone at the NHS primed his SAT-NAV and he duly announced we had arrived when in fact we were on an industrial estate outside a very large B & Q. He phoned in and was told the same thing had happened to someone else the previous day. We reprogrammed his SAT-NAV and arrived, via Richmond Park where we saw the red deer, in plenty of time to eat our lunch before we saw Professor Tom.

On entering his office, we found he had a couple of foreign neurologists with him. I had never been to see him with a walker before and he was surprised just how poor my co-ordination was. He was even more surprised when I asked him for the implant in my spine operation which had previously featured on the news. A lady in Canada had had it done. She had been in a wheelchair for five years because of her poor balance and freezing of gait and her many falls. After the operation she could walk unaided and did not even need a stick. Professor Tom told me that they did not do this operation. My response was that the NHNN was supposed to be the most prestigious hospital in the world so why were they not doing it. If Canada could do it and even Italy and France could do it, why not the NHNN, I had never been so forceful but was driven by the pain and the hopelessness of my situation.

Professor Tom looked quite piqued when I said this and, after a moment's reflection, he agreed with me. He said that he would speak to a lady surgeon, Professor Patricia Limousin about it, especially the risks of my coming off of the Pradaxa (blood thinners) and my chronic inflammatory arthritis. I replied that I was up for it whatever the risks as I would probably kill myself in one of my falls as they then numbered 86. He said he would telephone me in a couple of months or so to let me know what they had decided.

Meanwhile I showed him the letters from The Horder Centre.

Chapter 29- My Prediction Nearly Comes True

My falls have risen and now number 96. the last four have been the most spectacular and given me the most grief so far. On the fourth Tuesday in June we had our usual monthly Parky social. My Mum has taken to coming with us because afterwards we go shopping in Lidl before going home. On this occasion we had also brought with us two new residents from Sunrise Senior Living, a home for people with dementia and/or Parkinson's. My husband and I met them at a scrabble afternoon which we have been going to once a month for some time now at their request. It was decided that Mum and I would shop, and Mick would take this couple back to their home and then pick us up afterwards.

We did our shopping and I had paid for it when my festinating feet let me down and pitched me forward into the laps of two babies. In an effort to save myself from landing on them I grabbed the rail in front of them and the desk. Needless to say the two babies were not bothered and took the arrival of this lady flying down on them in their stride as they continued to munch on their bits of bread or whatever it was that their mum had given them. I got myself up somehow and apologised to the parents and went back to stand by my trolley. The mother followed me and asked me if I was OK. I told her it happened to me all the time and it was because I had Parkinson's. At that she told the cashier to immediately give me his chair which he did. I was enthroned upon it when my husband arrived, and my Mum came through with her shopping.

The following morning, I was very sore and stiff and on leaving my bedroom, heading off to singing, I fell again on the same left knee but this time landing on the metal strip between the carpets. That evening I discovered that my husband, having gone out for the evening, had left one of his heavy tool boxes outside and, as I thought it was going to rain, I went out to get it intending to leave it on the work surface in the utility room for him. I picked it up, turned round OK, arrived indoors OK, turned right and lifted his box up and down I went on my left knee again on the tiled floor. I did manage to keep the box on the work surface, though not completely, so I hastily shoved it on. My knee was already a mess but now my bruises had bruises on their bruises.

The final one of this run of falls occurred really as a result of these three. Friday evening came and I went up to run a bath. I only do this if Mick is home just in case I fall. I had always had no trouble getting in and out of the bath. I got in alright but getting out this time was another matter. As I lifted my right leg out to join my left one it gave way. I fell back into the bath. With water going everywhere (fortunately I had already pulled the plug out and much had drained away) I banged my head on the window recess. I shouted out to Mick who duly raced up the stairs closely followed by Holly Dog who is very cagey about stairs and would rather use the lift. Mick helped me out and the following morning my face was very swollen, so we went to A&E.

At A&E they decided that the swelling on my face had something to do with the filling I had had at the dentist the previous day for which I was given very strong antibiotics. They X-Rayed my left knee to check if I had broken anything and they insisted upon giving me a CT Scan to establish whether or not there was any internal bleeding in my brain. We were there until 12.30. We had previously said that we would sell tickets for the grand draw at St Thomas a Becket school fete. This school was where our grandchildren, Nathaniel and Mia-Joan were attending. We were very worried as we were so late, but the word had gotten around and when we arrived, we found that several friends had rallied round to sell the tickets until we turned up.

Days later and my left leg was totally black from the bruises inflicted upon it and had swollen up particularly round the ankle. I was bleeding into my foot and the blood was just seeping out but was held in my foot because the skin was unbroken.

The Art of Falling Gracefully

One of these days I may well kill myself in an horrendous fall; so hurry up and telephone me please.......

Chapter 30 – Am I returned to the NHS or Not

Meanwhile I had changed GPs. I had registered a complaint about Doctors not being able to ask for MRI Scans which I argued should have been available for the doctor to ask for in such extreme cases as my own. The CCG had put a blanket ban on doctors requesting MRI Scans (most likely because too many were being requested) and I was determined to change this order so others do not have to suffer the same excruciating pain levels that I did. My new GP in Eastbourne is lovely and gives me plenty of time despite the fact she is part-time. It's really as if she feels my pain. She had put in a request for physio for my spondylolisthesis (yes, I know it's a bit of a mouthful) and further she had requested my return to the NHS from the MSK people who control the waiting lists. We were getting very close to the July deadline before Dr. Tom Smith at Horders closed his list. We passed this deadline and I phoned MSK to see what was going on. They informed me that they had not received any request for me to go back to the NHS. I was absolutely livid because my pain levels were at an all-time high but had now moved to the right side as I had had a fall but this time, I crumpled my right leg under me.

My new GP approved my plan of action to increase the Gabapentin to the hospital level of 600 mg in the morning, 300 mg in the afternoon and 900 mg in the evening. While this worked to a certain extent, I was also prescribed a large bottle of Oramorphine to be taken as needed but not exceeding four times a day and the dose was between 2.5 and 5 ml. At first, I found myself using it 2-3 times a day. In the morning I took a little dose of 2.5 ml and on bad days a similar top up in the afternoon. In the evening I took a 5 ml dose. Later on, I changed this to 5 ml in the morning and 5 ml in the evening and this worked much better for me. Sometimes when going to Hydrotherapy I feel the pain bubbling up so I add in a 2.5 ml so I can last the distance. To date I have gone through just under a litre and a half.

About this time Horders rang me and asked why I had not kept the appointment made for that morning, I replied I went to see Dr. Tom Smith earlier just after the hospital had upped the Gabapentin and he said he would cancel the two other check-ups that were on the books. Horders asked me how I was getting on with swapping back to the NHS and I explained what had happened and said I would probably miss the schedule for August whenever that was. Right she said I will contact the MSK people for you. I will give you a ring in a day or two.

Ten minutes later she was back on the phone.
"Mrs Lees" she said
"Yes" I said
"You are back on the NHS." She said I would be on the list on 26th September. More information would be

sent nearer the time. It duly arrived and everything was sorted out. I put the phone down and just shouted," Mick, I am back on the NHS and I'm on the September list". "What" he said as he emerged from the bathroom, "What did you say". So I repeated it for him.

However, the fates were either against me or for me as the day before the 26th the surgeon must have gone sick because they cancelled my injections until 14th October. They were doomed never to take place.

Chapter 31 – To See or Not to See That is the Question

Now one Sunday morning I don't remember whether it was in July or August but everywhere I looked I saw a rather large black spot. It started when I was washing my hands in the sink and there was a distinct black spot at least a centimetre across. When I looked elsewhere the spot was there as well. So, we made another trip to the A&E in the DGH.

After a short wait, drops were put in my eyes and we went to see the DGH's eye man. After examining my eyes, he said it's nothing to worry about. I was told that it was just a vitreous detachment but if it gets any bigger it could pull the retina off the back of my eye. So, if I see something like a curtain coming down, I was to go back as soon as possible.

It so happens that Dr Clare (my niece) who I have mentioned before, texted me to see how I was getting on. I told her what had happened that morning and she must have told her father because the next thing I knew he was on the phone telling me that the retina in his left eye had fallen off two weeks ago and he could not go on holiday with his family but was coming down to Eastbourne to stay with Mum for a few days. I told him not to worry her with my eyesight problems.

Why not I hear you ask. Well several years previously, in 1982, my Mum, crazy woman that she is, drove herself to Mayday Hospital Eye Unit as both of her retinas were falling off. Just as she pulled up in the street where the eye unit was, she went totally blind. She called for help and a kind passer-by helped her into the eye unit. From there she phoned me to say could my husband, who just happened to be working close by that day come and check that she had suitably parked her car (it was parked right in the middle of the road but we will gloss over her driving skills) and could I find my Dad and tell him what had happened. (What would have happened if her retinas had completely come away whilst she was driving does not bear thinking about and I told her in no uncertain terms that she should either have phoned for an ambulance or got a taxi!)

Find my Dad in London – Good grief that was going to be a nigh on impossible task. You see my Dad was a Lloyds Broker who was well known and trusted at Lloyds. He would leave his slips with one underwriter who would pass them onto the next until 100% of the risk was taken up. Dad would either return to the office or go and talk to other brokers or have his lunch in a pub.

After two and a half hours of searching I eventually found him, and he immediately left everything and jumped in a cab arriving about half an hour later. In those days they used a laser to stick the retinas back on but only one of Mum's retinas was successfully put back; from the other eye she said she just saw hazy light and the shapes of people and things. Luckily, we had moved to a new house early that summer so that my eldest, Andrew, could get to The John Fisher School in Purley. We did not have a problem with Debbie as she would get into Coloma Convent Girls School in Shirley because that was my old school. So, Dad used to deliver Mum to me in the morning, as she could not see well yet and the kids entertained her whilst I got on with the chores.

Now if anyone mentions eye problems, she just freaks out so the less said the better I told my brother. As it was, she had a go at me when Francis invited himself to stay with her.

"Why didn't you tell me" she hissed in my ear.

"Because I didn't know until a couple of days before you, and I know what you are like. You won't sleep. It will go to your stomach. You'll feel sick all the time and you won't eat either."

"Oh dear I hope my detachment behaves itself but I think if has increased very slightly."

Chapter 32 – East Grinstead and then London Again

A few days later the phone rang again and this time it was the admissions unit of the NHNN. Would I come up on the 2nd October and expect to be in overnight and home the next day as they wanted me to do the Levodopa Challenge again with me totally off my Parkinson's medication.

But first I had to face my rheumatologist on 1st October. It was pouring with rain and many of the roads were flooded so we had to go quite slowly as we did not want to aquaplane. We arrived in plenty of time, and as the person in front of me did not keep his/her appointment, I was seen almost immediately. I was weighed and measured, and the nurse said 5 feet 5 inches to herself.

I said to her "That's not correct I was 5 feet 6 inches at school, and I grew half an inch having my three children". My youngest, Adam, was born about a year after Mum's eye problems. The nurse measured me again.

"Yes, I am still right 5 feet and 5 inches," she said.

I wondered to myself whether that was because I had early disc degeneration of my spine as I have been told, in the past, that my spine looked like that of an old builder who had carried and shovelled far too much muck about in his working life. Looking back, I did shovel a load of concrete when I was eighteen as my parents decided to lay the concrete plinth for a rather large shed instead of getting a builder in to do it; Also when we moved, for the sake of the future schooling of the children, my husband moved in on crutches, as he had some cartilage removed in one of his knees and we had to make a safe path for the kids who were then just 5 and 2. We also had to take up a 20 foot long higgledy piggledy patio and relay with flagstones. As my husband discovered after the bandages were removed from his knee that he could no longer kneel down to do these jobs it fell on my shoulders to do them as we were thoroughly skint and could not afford to employ a builder.

Dr. Makadsi started by examining my hands and was very pleased with the result as there was no longer any sign of the swollen knuckles and he asked me if I had any pain in them to which I replied "No, not anymore," but I had a lot of bother with my left shoulder. He suggested that I have a steroid injection in it and produced a long needle and a phial of stuff. It had worked on my knee, so I promptly agreed. I knew if I relaxed it would not hurt, so I did, and it didn't. He turned to my husband and said, "You know your wife is a very brave lady." As I was adjusting my clothing at the time, I missed an opportunity to reply

He told me to continue with the medications as prescribed and he would see me in 10 months. We left his office and I calmed down as I had been inwardly shaking that he might have wanted to examine my knees which were still a multi-shade of black, purple, green and red. Remember when you bruise yourself the bruise is a bleed and I go on for weeks seeping blood. I think it was because I came in with my walker and Mick helped me into the chair that he thought she is behaving herself!

The next day the patient transport arrived or rather a taxi hired by patient transport did. The driver duly explained that when there were too many calls, they employed taxi drivers. He duly put my suitcase in the back with me and my walker in his boot and off we went. Now Mick always goes in the front of cars because he is dreadfully car sick as a general rule. Anyway, we hit the one-way system in London and boy-o-boy he certainly could ride the brakes on his car. I had been dozing before, but it definitely woke my stomach up.

With a mile to go I said you had better stop and I had no sooner got out the car than up it came. We all got back in about a quarter of an hour later when my stomach had stopped heaving and made it to the NHNN without any further incident. I asked Mick if he was OK and he said he had never felt so rotten and wasn't he a dreadful driver riding his brake like that and stopping and starting every couple of inches.

The Art of Falling Gracefully

Anyway, we arrived on the ward to discover my bed wasn't ready, so we went to the small day room attached to another ward. Whilst waiting around and kicking our heels, a nurse came and said I was wanted downstairs to record my speech. I had done this all before, so it was no surprise. Again, I don't know if it was tiredness or the pain I was in but my voice was very low and I had to shout but in reality when I was shouting, I was talking in my usual voice. After doing all his tests and it didn't take long. I went back to the ward and was able to settle in. I have to say that the staff could not have been more attentive. Cups of tea appeared from nowhere, and there was plenty of choice on the menu.

I was then taken down to see Professor Limousin's assistant, a young lady Doctor who I think had Chinese origins, who explained what was going to happen in the morning. After she had finished, I told her I had done this all before and Mick piped up saying why was it necessary to do it all over again. The doctor explained to him that, when anyone was considered for surgery with Parkinson's, they had to establish exactly how bad they were, so they had a comparison of "before and after." At this point Mick had to leave to get home to rescue Holly Dog from my Mum who tended to spoil her somewhat, which is why Holly Dog likes to go there.

Chapter 33- Preparing for The Levodopa Challenge

The rest of that day I was reminded constantly that I should not take any of my Parkinson's medication after 10 o'clock. Even during the night when I asked for a dose of morphine, they still reminded me as they had left me to self-medicate. The morphine being a controlled substance had to be taken under their wing.

Inevitably dawn came following a totally sleepless night as a male member of staff insisted upon talking at the top of his voice and the lady next to me was in dreadful pain and she refused to try certain medications that would have helped her. So between the two of them sleep evaded me. At 6 o'clock, fearful that I would not be able to shower on my own, and, after having taken just my usual antihistamine which I always began the day with, I went to the shower room. I managed very well and returned to be asked if I wanted tea or coffee with my toast. I replied, "Black tea please." as I was told to have no dairy. Toast arrived with marmalade and, you guessed it, butter on the side.

I was asked if I had had any Parkinson's medication to which I replied no just my antihistamine and I was going to take my Gabapentin, Pradaxa (blood thinners) and the Hydroxychloroquine for my inflammatory arthritis.

The Art of Falling Gracefully

A short time later a porter appeared like magic with a wheelchair to whisk me away. He bought it right up beside me and I nipped across into it and we were off. However before we could escape someone else asked about my Parkinson's medication to which I replied "Only my antihistamine, Gabapentin, Pradaxa and Hydroxychloroquine" I replied as the porter took me down to the basement for the challenge, where for the last time (Thank God) I was asked if I had had any Parkinson's medication after 10 o'clock last night. I just said quietly "No". I knew I would be asked one more time.

Chapter 34– The Battle Commences

The same Chinese doctor, a lovely lady, was going to look after me. She had given me various questionnaires the night before to fill in about my Parkinson's, but she said Professor Limousin would wish to go through them with me later. At this point she appeared and said she would come along when I was walking without medication just to see how I was." Ok" we both said. The doctor thought I had not "gone off enough" so we had to wait a bit. About an hour later I was shaking and in a right state. "Good" she said, "Into my office" and a porter duly pushed me inside her office. The tests are not hard when you are normal but can be exceedingly frustrating when you are tremoring and cannot control your legs, arms, feet or hands.

The first test was the easiest but even so I failed it miserably. There were two thumb prints of ink about a foot apart on her desk and I had to use one finger and go from one thumb print to the other as quickly as possible Needless to say I was slow on the right side but I just about managed it 50% of the time but with my left hand I was totally hopeless. Next, I had to do the finger flapping which my left hand decided not to do at all. This was all videoed for posterity so that new doctors could learn how bad unmedicated Parkinson's could be. Eventually we came to walking and right on time Professor Limousin popped her head round the door. "I'll just stay to watch this "she said.

First of all, I had to get up out of the chair. Could I get up without using the arms of the chair to lever myself up. (We had been practising this one in the gym, so I knew exactly what to do). On the tenth attempt I gave up and had to use the arms of the chair to lever myself up. I staggered very slowly across the floor, more of a shuffle than a walk and two feet from the door my legs froze, stuck to the floor as if they had been super-glued. We all chanted one, two, one, two........ I asked someone to sing as that usually worked..... but my feet still refused to move. They tried me with a line across the floor for me to step over..... nothing doing and my feet remained glued.

I am convinced that my legs thought the gap was too small.

In the end, after about ten minutes, Professor Limousin and her assistant had to drag me through the door with my feet resisting every step of the way.

Once she had me in the corridor the Professor asked me to walk up the corridor. Unlike last time when the surgeon had to belt up the corridor to catch me as I fell over, she accompanied me with her assistant. We only walked a few yards when she asked me to stop and turn around. She had to help me to turn around.

116

The Art of Falling Gracefully

Then I shuffled back the way I had come. One of the doctor's assistants then produced, like a rabbit out of a hat, a wheelchair saying she could not bear to see me go through the same procedure again getting back into the doctor's office. So I was wheeled back into her office and was helped back into the chair.

Professor Limousin said she would come back to see me again once I was back "on." Last time I was given 100 mg of dispersible Madopar and you may recall that I was still not fully "on", one and a half hours later so they gave me 150 mg this time. I was taken, again in my wheelchair, to wait in the corridor and, after a little while, the Professor parked herself in the chair next to me and said she thought that I was a prime candidate for the implant to my spine but as we have to do these things under the auspices of pain management she advised me not to have the injections planned for later that month. So I agreed that I would not.

After half an hour we went back into the office and we repeated the whole thing all over again. Needless to say, I managed everything well except my walking where I was a bit hesitant for about a minute.

At the end the doctor said to me that I was one of the most relaxed persons she had seen doing the tests. Many people had to do it over two days as they got so stressed. The Professor said she would arrange for me to come up to London to meet the team who would look after me and said she would contact me very soon.

Chapter 35 – To Be In Pain Or Not To Be In Pain

Thinking that things would move along quite quickly, I telephoned Dr Tom Smith's secretary and explained everything to her. She informed me that as a fall back I had until 20th January 2020 to come back to her or I had to be referred back to my GP. I thanked her and then a couple of days later I fell over on my butt in the house in the lounge. I knew something had happened because the next morning I was in terrible agony down my right leg the pain started in the bottom of my spine and wave after wave of excruciating pain wafted down my leg.

After a couple of weeks, I went onto my patient records at the UCLH and wrote to Dr Limousin to tell her what had happened. She said she would press the other members attending and we went up on the 6th November, again in a taxi paid for by patient transport. The journey up this time was fine and we arrived with 10 minutes or so to spare. Promptly five minutes after my interview should have started, Professor Tom put his head around the door and invited Mick and me in. I was introduced to Dr. Harith Akram, who was a spine surgeon. He told me that they had gotten hold of my MRI Scan that I had paid for at Horder and it wasn't very clear, but it gave them a reasonable idea of what was going on. I told them that I had been in the MRI scanner with my legs held up very high without any pain killing medication for about an hour and a half in

119

all. They were up on some sort of plastic thing which was shoved next to my butt. As they were nearing the end of the first session, the scanning of my spine I hit the panic button and told them I was in dire straits as my left leg was in total agony; their response was to shove the end of a very thin blanket over the bench which succeeded in diminishing the pain by zero.

True to their word they finished the scanning in the allotted 5 minutes and returned with what resembled a very thick piece of paper in a sort of "T"-shape. This they said was to fit my torso so I remained still while they did the scan of my hips; I remember that I didn't like the look of it one bit as it reminded me of a large piece of plaster board (which I am very familiar with having had builders in and out of the house for six years since we moved down to Eastbourne).

I asked them if it would hurt. "No" they replied you will just perhaps feel a little pressure. So they put it on me. Immediately I felt such pain that it was near impossible to describe except that it felt like I was being stabbed a thousand times in my hips and along my back. I heard someone screaming and the scanning crew returned to whip off the board. It was only later that I realised that I was the one who had been screaming.

They then completed the scan and I went home. So that is why the scan is not clear!

The Art of Falling Gracefully

At this point the memory became too much and I burst into tears. Offers of tissues from all sides came and the questions continued but we were on safer ground here, or so they all thought, as Dr Akram asked why I was no longer on ropinirole. I explained what had happened and that the neurologist I had seen in Eastbourne did not want me to experience that again, so I was on antihistamines for life. I was also asked about the blood thinners so again I explained what had happened.

My pain levels were also discussed, and I said they were down to a dull ache but considering the number of painkillers I was taking they were surprised that I had any pain at all.

I again had to show off my walking skills which proved to be laughable, without my walker or my stick as once again my feet declared that doorway gaps were too small etc.

Anyway, the upshot was that I would have an MRI Scan repeated just on the lumbar region of my spine. I would then have an operation to relieve the pain from the spondylolisthesis and when Professor Limousin said that I was still on the list for the spinal implant I very nearly cried again as I thought it would never happen.

The Art of Falling Gracefully

We left the NHNN at 4.15 p.m. and sat and had something to eat before we called our taxi driver to take us home which turned out to be a nightmare journey. We took 2 and three quarter of an hour to get there but it took four hours to get us home. Getting out of London is a positive nightmare in the rush hour traffic and, despite the driver being a very good one, he had to stop twice for me to get out and throw up!!!!

Chapter 36- UCLH and MyCare

Once I was back at home and had rested, I looked through the various pieces of correspondence which I had been given. I found a section saying that they had started an initiative on the Internet so patients could see when their next appointments were, test results etc. etc. So following the given instructions I logged on and found myself. There in black and white were my next appointments 3rd January with Professor Tom for my Parkinson's and 24th January for the appointment with Dr. Akram. I was disappointed for one minute as they did say that they would try to marry both appointments on the same day. Also, there was no sign of the new MRI Scan.

Meanwhile my falls had gone up to 124 and the 125th was fairly interesting although it was the worst one for the pain. I came out of my en-suite bathroom and turned round to turn the light off and, I don't know how it happened, but I fell against the sharp edge of the ottoman box. It made contact with my spine from the bottom all the way up. Now I have always prided myself in not waking my husband on my nocturnal wanderings but this time my mouth opened, and I emitted an awful scream. Mick shot bolt upright in bed calling my name, wondering where I was and, worse, Holly Dog had been woken from a deep sleep in the kitchen and started barking.....furiously.

The Art of Falling Gracefully

Mick's question was of course a stupid one as I was whimpering in pain at the foot of the bed. It was a wonder that one of the neighbours did not call the police out. Mick came to help me get up, but I said no just in case I had broken something. I managed, within a few minutes, to turn myself over onto my knees and very slowly I got up. My back felt a bit easier, so I gradually finished my return journey to bed with Holly Dog still barking but not in quite such a frenetic way as before.

Mick covered me over and went down to shut our small, furry beast up before she woke the whole neighbourhood. By this time, I was fast asleep again. For the next couple of days, I wandered about the house in a daze thinking my back had improved but had not said anything to Mick.

Two days later as I was walking round the dining room table my legs gave way again and I found myself huddled in a small space after I had banged the side of my head on a small but very decorative cupboard. Mick was out at the time and when he returned, he wondered whether or not I should go for a CT Scan. I replied no because I had done it 5 hours ago and if I had had a bleed, I would have had a stroke or at least a small TIA by then.

With my back being a little better I thought I would try doing some dusting. I managed this but had to sit down exhausted but feeling quite pleased, this being the first "job" I had managed since I fell 12 months previously.

Mick caught me with duster in hand and asked me what I was doing. I then explained that the fall that I had had in the bedroom must have corrected something because the pain was not so bad suddenly. (Even so I was still on Gabapentin, Paracetamol and Oramorphine as well as one Ibuprofen for my inflammatory arthritis which had flared up quite considerably now that the weather had changed to being cold with rain every day.)

.

Chapter 37– I Wet Myself Again and Holly Dog has an Operation

The Parkinson's November social arrived and with it the Recycled Band who played for just their expenses. Any profits they made went to charity. We always have them at the November social which tends to be packed out. One of the band was diagnosed with Parkinson's about a year before and goes to Hailsham Parkinson's group which Mick and I joined as we used to go bowling with them. You may recall I had a spectacular fall at the leisure centre in front of the Hailsham bowlers.

Mick now bowls with Eastbourne Senior Rollers every Tuesday, after Robert Taylor suggested he join, and does not normally get back until well after 1 o'clock. He usually has his lunch before the social starts as I pack him a little lunch box to eat once we get there. This time he managed to eat it before we set off.

We arrived about half an hour before kick-off at 2 o'clock with a somewhat subdued Holly Dog with a lampshade around her head. Everyone wanted to know what had happened, so I told them that she had had an operation on the left side of her head the day before.

She had caught what the vet called a wart from another dog which had reached a certain size and then Holly Dog must have knocked or scratched the top off. Anyway, she had a one-centimetre hole on the left side of her face just under her left ear. I found a second hole just northwest of the first one the day before she had her op. Why did we not spot it before, we were asked. I replied that I always brush her at night time when she sits on my lap and watches the TV for her little films (the adverts) as she invariably barks at them because ten to one there is a dog in them. She did have a shocking skin complaint which we keep under control washing her twice a week if it gets bad with Vosene and then a dog shampoo afterwards, so she regains her dog ph on her skin. So my brushing includes a massage (so I can keep an eye on her skin condition) and then a good comb out of her back.

Her face which she resolutely keeps on the TV in case Harvey, or Sykes, as he is known as in Midsomer Murders, appears as she is potty about him. So I never get to see her face and assume Mick deals with it in the morning; but I forgot that she sits on her towel in her room on the draining board next to the Belfast sink which we use as her bath and always faces the kitchen so Mick never sees the left side properly. Holly dog has had her check-ups and was doing very well. We will be dispensing with the lampshade in a about a week.

I digress......

The Art of Falling Gracefully

After the social we went shopping in Aldi as we needed bread and milk but came away with a mountain of stuff as does everyone else. We returned to the car when, hey ho down I went. Did I forget to say it was raining and Mick was parked next to an Olympic size puddle which I landed in. Somehow the water cushioned the blow as it seeped into my padded jacket which then seeped into my jogging pants which in turn seeped into my knickers. A man came rushing to help me to get up just as I realised that this was one time when I could never get up by myself. Mick waved the man away saying he could manage. I smiled and told him it happens all the time. It was just my Parkinson' s and I fall over regularly.

Chapter 38 – Mother sees me fall again

My 128th fall came about doing a good deed for my Mum. She is a keen gardener, even at 91 and she had been on the lookout for lawn sand as her lawns in the back garden were dreadfully full of moss. We were in ESK, a local warehouse which sells just about everything and I thought we would just see if they had any. So Mick beetled off and appeared seconds later struggling with a very large bag. "Is it?" said I but got no further as he smiled and said "Yes."

It was our intention to go round early on Sunday night to deliver it before Mick took Mum and I to church for Holy Mass. I cannot manage to be up in time for the 9.15 Mass at St. Gregory's, but Mick manages to get there as he has reading and ministerial duties. We arrived and I went around to open the latch at the top of the gate, but I could not quite reach it with my arms aching as they were. I moved onto the lawn and down I went on Mum's nicely resined drive tripping over a slightly raised edging around the grass. I grazed both of my knees but otherwise escaped unharmed even managing to keep my head up so I didn't smash my teeth like last time. Mick helped me up from the damp grass and sat me down in the car.

Mum got in the back and had a bit of a shock when she saw Holly Dog with her lampshade around her head. We had not told Mum about Holly Dog's operation as we did not want to worry her. I then told her that Holly Dog had had an operation to close two holes on her face caused by the warts she had scratched off. She was doing very well and she would lose the lampshade next Thursday.

I asked Mum to look for the scrapings from my knees in daylight !!!!

Like Queen Victoria, she was not amused.

Chapter 39 – Another MRI Scan

Inevitably the morning came, and a letter dropped down on my doorstep telling me to attend at Bulstrode Place for an MRI Scan that would be conducted by Alliance Medical who carry out a large number of MRI Scan's for the NHNN. However, the letter continued that if we required patient transport we had to ring and let them know because you could not get it to Bulstrode Place. Why? You may ask.!!! Anyway, more of that later.

I telephoned the NHNN and they said that they would send me an appointment to have it done there. Inevitably, Alliance Medical rang me to give me another appointment and I said that I could not attend there as I needed patient transport from Eastbourne and back. Can you arrange it for yourself I was asked? I replied in the affirmative, but I was told in the letter giving me the first appointment that it was not possible to use their facility if you were using patient transport. I was then informed that if I could get my patient transport organised, they could see me on 10 December at 12.30 p.m. I agreed and Mick promptly phoned the patient transport team to arrange for us to be picked up, taken to Bulstrode Place and returned home. I received, a couple of days later, an appointment for an MRI Scan at the NHNN for a date about a week later, but at 7.00 in the morning.

The Art of Falling Gracefully

You are joking!!!

Exasperated with the appointment makers at the NHNN I rang and told them that Alliance Medical had rung with another date and because we were organising our own transport, we could have it done there. Besides I would never make their early one as I am very slow in the mornings. In reality I would have had to get up shower and breakfast and be ready to leave at four in the morning which meant getting out of bed at 2 am. No way could I do that.

Well the day eventually arrived and, with Holly Dog safely delivered to my Mum for the day, another taxi arrived and when I opened the door the driver said "Good Morning Veronika" I looked at him closely and it was the same driver, whose name was Joe as we discovered, we had had for our last trip. En route, the driver told us that he had been a black cabbie in London before he came to Eastbourne and, as a result, when his SAT-NAV showed him where the next blockage was, he ducked around it. As a result, we had a wonderful tour of Dulwich village.

This time it was Mick's turn to throw up again as he had not taken his Kwells for travel sickness, but we managed to get there. I had barely sat down in Bulstrode Place before I was called in. They could not have been nicer people. As I had my walker with me, they showed me to a cubicle big enough to remove any clothing with metal in it and any jewellery which I left there under lock and key.

I had to leave my walker outside the scanning room, but two ladies offered me their arms to make sure I did not fall over making my way to the bed. They helped me on and made sure that I was very comfortable but unfortunately my feet could not stay still. I suggested that they tie my legs up with something; so, they got hold of a couple of very soft blankets and carefully wrapped my tremoring legs up and then strapped them down. They asked if I felt any discomfort, to which I replied, "No" and that I was quite comfortable. What a difference compared with Horder's attitude. After giving me earplugs and earmuffs with some nice music playing, they left the room.

The MRI scanner started up and every few minutes they broke into the music and asked me if I was OK. After 20 minutes the machine stopped, and they told me that they were just checking for the quality of pictures and to make sure that they had caught everything requested. A minute or two later the two ladies came back and helped me off the scanner after unbuckling my legs and taking all the blankets off.

I shifted around and once the bed was lowered which they did very slowly they both helped me to my feet. Once I was steady I was ushered unhurriedly to the door and with walker back in hand I made my way back to the cubicle to redress myself and rescue all the bits I had left in the lockable cupboard. When I was fully ready, I sat outside and only waited a couple of minutes before one of the ladies escorted me downstairs to meet up with Mick again. We sat and had some lunch and then called the taxi man back.

The journey home proved to be fairly reasonable when you consider we left at about 2.30 p.m. we missed most of the worse traffic and we ended up going home by a route we certainly knew from the M25 down the A22 to Eastbourne. I was quite tired by this time and slept most of the way home.

The Christmas festivities were upon us and my choir was in demand. We sang at a new nursing home, Beechwood Grove, on 13th November followed on 20th November by singing for about 40 minutes at our wonderful hospice St. Wilfred's where our Parkinson's nurse, Becky, had organised a Parkinson's Awareness Day for carers. On 11th December we gave a Christmas Concert to the residents of Bernhard Baron Cottage Homes, a Quaker foundation in Polegate, where once again we were asked to come back so we arranged to return in June 2020 and once more they presented me with a lovely card and, on opening it, £70 fell out again!

We sang at our own social on 17th December for

about 45 minutes and then we fell upon the tea party we had organised. Much talk was stopped as we all filled our plates and then transferred what we had chosen to our mouths.

On the 18th we had our Christmas lunch and about 64 people ended up sitting round tables at the Langham Hotel, which in my view has the best food in town. Our Group had received a legacy of £5,000 to spend. Nearly half of it was set aside to support the hydrotherapy group and the singing unit and the balance paid for the Christmas social tea party where every attendee was given a large round box of sweets. Further the Christmas Lunch was paid for those who regularly attended the socials and was partly subsidised for others. For entertainment, Ben the 15-year old son of our singing teacher sang for everyone.

It was an excellent way to finish 2019. Everyone said how much they had enjoyed it. Little did we appreciate how our lives would be changed just a few short weeks later.

Chapter 40- All is revealed

I had a letter telling me to visit with Dr Akram at the National Hospital for Integrated Medicine the "NHIM" which is on the third floor of the NHNN on the 24th January to discuss the results of the MRI Scan and to make a decision on what to do next, As it was over a month away and I was not feeling too bad, we made a hasty retreat to Leeds booking ourselves and Holly Dog into the Best Western and Milford Hotel which was only a couple of miles from where our son Adam lives with his wife Bronwen and the children Joshua and Isabella or Izzy for short.

We left on the 11th January to travel up over two days just in case my back played up staying at the Days Inn near Peterborough with Holly Dog overnight. Nearly every day we visited with Adam and his wife Bronwen and Josh who, at the age of 10 is not so little anymore (well his Father is 6 feet 3 inches tall) and Izzy who still squeaks when she gets excited. On Friday 17th we went to see the house that Bronwen's parents had purchased a couple of years ago which was just around the corner. Their garden backed onto Adam's but is three gardens to the right. I am glad they moved to be near them as they had no family in the surrounding area. We left the following day again staying in the same Days Inn at Peterborough on the way home. It was an excellent break, but I was very tired when we got home.

The Art of Falling Gracefully

My appointment with Dr Akram was at 2.30 p.m. We had a different driver this time, but we soon settled down with him. From the outset he said if you need to stop for whatever reason just let me know. He was a very kind gentleman. If I remember correctly, we arrived this time without incident as Mick had remembered to take his travel sickness pills and I just fell asleep. We found Dr. Akram's clinic and settled down to wait. It was not long before he was calling my name as he came to fetch me. He looked just like a schoolboy. "God" I thought "He is so young" or should it rather be "God I am so old". We entered his office and I saw straight away that he had my MRI Scan up on screen. He told me it was a very clear picture this time and he could see quite clearly where my spinal cord was being pinched. He said that I had two options:-

Option A- was to do nothing, or

Option B - surgical intervention to decompress my spinal cord so it was no longer pinched, and I should be pain free. The operation involved the removal of the knob that you can feel going down your spine at lumber 4 together with the two arms that attach it to the rest of the vertebra.

However, he did explain that there were some risks with the operation. He could nick the dura or sheath covering the cord which would mean I would have to lie flat on my back for two days or so while it healed or it may require a pump to soak up the leakage from the spinal cord or his scalpel could slip and I could end up never walking again or I could end up with a bit of permanent "on and off" back pain.

I told him that I could not continue on my pain killing regime. As it was my weight was beginning to seesaw so I told him I would have the operation please, as to do nothing was not an option. I thought to myself if Professor Tom says he is the best in the business he must be good, and I have a lot of faith in Professor Tom. He told me the operation was called a laminectomy which I got Mick to write down so I could look it up on the Internet later. My writing is now so bad I might as well not bother.

He said I would have to see the anaesthetist beforehand because I was on Dabigatran Etexilate (Pradaxa or blood thinners) and because of the Methotrexate which is a chemo-therapy drug which does prevent healing, but in small doses is very beneficial for chronic inflammatory arthritis. He said he would just pop and see if the anaesthetist could see me that afternoon; but he returned very quickly to say that he was fully booked. If possible, he would schedule me for the 13th March (The sooner the better I thought) and if I came in for 7 a.m. in the morning that day... he got no further. I told him that that was an impossible thing for me to do. First my

Parkinson's makes me extremely slow in the mornings so I would have to be up at 2 a.m. to be sure of being ready for Patient Transport to arrive at 4 a.m. and then I would be throwing up all the way on route as I could have nothing by mouth. He looked astonished and asked me where I lived. Mick and I replied in unison "We live in Eastbourne on the South Coast". "I see your problem. You had better come in the night before then." "Thank you" I said, and we left.

I was told that once we reached the M25 I fell asleep again. We arrived home about 6.30 and Mick went to rescue Holly Dog from Mum once he had had a cup of tea and I had phoned her to tell her what was happening.

Chapter 41– I Re-Christen Holly Dog

I think that it was the following Monday I had my next fateful fall. It was fateful for many reasons. But first of all, I had better tell you what usually happens on a Monday. Mick volunteers in the chaplaincy at the DGH every Monday and leaves home about 9.30 a.m. but has to be back promptly at 1 p.m. to take me to hydrotherapy again at the DGH. Holly Dog is quite used to this regime and invariably waits for something to eat until Mick brings her home after dropping me off.

This particular Monday Holly decided she wanted her din-dins before we went. So I went to her fridge and got her bowl out with the odd biscuit in it left from breakfast, took off the cover and turned around.

My feet glued themselves to the spot, but my body carried forward. I flung Holly Dog's bowl on the work surface (where it stayed – fortunately!!) and made a grab at the work surface in an effort to stop myself from falling. I raked the edge of it with my nails and that was all. I hit the work surface on the wooden edge across the right side of my jaw, across my chin and part of my neck before I bounced back and hit the right side of my head again on the sharp edge of the work surface, before ending up in a dazed heap on the floor, in a corner. The thought of getting up terrified me as I had to have done some damage, so I sat there a few

140

minutes with Holly Dog looking at me quite disdainfully as if saying;-

"OK, enough of your play acting now. Where's my din-dins?"

A few minutes later and I was still just sitting there when it occurred to me that Mick was late......... so I had to try to get up but I wanted to get up on a soft surface just in case my legs did not support me. So I slowly bum shuffled (yes bum shuffled just like a baby does and at the age of 68 as well. How undignified!!!) my way through the length of the kitchen until I hit the lounge doorway where I carried on until I got to the wooden end of a leather sofa where I managed eventually, after several false starts, to pull myself up and collapse onto the seat.

I suddenly felt awful pain in my cheek, and I winced on touching it especially underneath my chin. By this time, it was a quarter past one and still no sign of Mick, so I rang his mobile only to hear it ringing in the hall. I think it was my lowest point ever. I muttered under my breathe "As for you Holly Dog, we should change your name to "Holly the Pest of a Dog."

Mick eventually arrived home at 1.25 p.m. After one of the patient's died at the hospital. He had never been so late. He said he could still get me to hydrotherapy if I was ready to go now as he came in through the front door. To which I replied we were definitely going to the DGH but not to hydrotherapy. He turned the corner into the lounge, and I lowered the paper I had been hiding behind. He paled visibly.

"A&E?" "Most definitely" and I explained what had happened. He fed Holly the Pest of a Dog and let her out in the garden for a few minutes whilst he helped me into the car. Soon after, leaving Holly the Pest of a Dog in her basket in the kitchen, we were off arriving just five minutes later.

We stopped at hydrotherapy and Mick popped in to tell them what had happened. We continued onwards. At reception I explained that I had banged my head and my jaw, but I was concerned as I was on blood thinners. She told me to take a seat in the waiting area. As my legs were shaking Mick had bought me into the hospital in a wheelchair. Two minutes later and I had jumped the queue to see the triage nurse who went to get a doctor to have a look at me. The doctor didn't think I had broken anything, but he got a porter to whip me down for a CT Scan. I only waited a couple of minutes before I was taken to the CT Scanner. A CT Scanner can do in a few minutes what an MRI Scanner takes to do in about 15 minutes or so.

After the CT Scan was completed, we waited a couple of minutes for a porter who dragged me backwards up to the waiting area (why is it that NHS wheelchairs are so cumbersome and, even when new, cannot be pushed. I also wondered if they had ever lost a patient who just fell off). On arrival in the waiting area we were called in just five minutes later to see another doctor who also examined me where the bruising was yellow, red and green all over my right cheek and bright red and black under and around my chin. He concurred with the first doctor that he did not think I had broken my jaw. He also told me that I had not had a bleed in my brain, and I had to go home and rest.

We left passing the hydrotherapy unit just as Debbie Soaves the head physiotherapist came out. She took one look at my face and demanded that I accept motorised transport around the house. She said she would arrange for the NHS to get in touch. I meekly said "OK" as by then it was getting difficult to talk. But I was determined at the same time not to have some big, difficult to move, wheelchair. I wanted a small one that would also go up and down as well so I could reach all my top cupboards.

Every day for a week thereafter I gracefully sank to the floor as my legs gave way underneath.

Chapter 42 – East Grinstead Again

Over the past few weeks my arms had begun to ache which gradually got so bad the tears would roll down my cheeks whenever I had to dress or undress so much so that Mick was helping me every day into my undergarments and shirts and jumpers. When it came to putting a coat on it was nightmare time. With my arms in this state I agreed that I needed to see my rheumatologist as a matter of urgency. So I rang his secretary and explained that I was in such dreadful pain I could not wait for the next appointment in August. She double booked Dr. Makadsi on Tuesday 4th February at 2 p.m. and asked me to be there at 1.45 p.m.

We arrived in plenty of time and the nurse called me in to weigh and measure me and then told me to sit on one of the chairs outside his office. I had no sooner sat down than I was called in. I explained in detail what was happening, and he said it sounded as if I was having a flare up. Anyway, he looked at my record on his computer in disgust as he could not see any blood test results. He asked me to bring the results with me next time I went to see him. The NHS tried to put in a computer system so that your records could be read at any hospital in the UK but although their intention was good it never worked, which is why Dr. Makadsi could not access my blood test results on my records.

Anyway, he gave me a short course of steroids and told me to keep the next regular appointment. On taking the steroids it was three days before I felt any better and when I cut them down for the second week, I felt the rippling of pain just below the surface.

As soon as I ran out of these little pills, the pain returned with a vengeance. There was no time to schedule another visit as my operation was just around the corner

Two weeks later and my face had healed reasonably well; I had expected it to take a bit longer. So I joined the choir singing at Coppice Court for the second time. Pat the lady who sorts out the activities, apologised for not sending a cheque to me for the first time we sang there last year and handed me an envelope with £60 in it. We had sung at JPK, a community Drop-In Centre, the previous month and picked up another booking at a new home (well to us it was) called Grange House Residential Home. As Mick and I had to go into town we went to visit this new place and met with the entertainment manager and confirmed we would be there on 13th May.

The following Sunday Mick arranged for my Parish Priest to come round to give me the Seventh Sacrament - the Anointing of the Sick. Fr. Raglan telephoned me the next day to say he could come after he had done his refresher on sign language in

The Art of Falling Gracefully

Crawley. He reckoned he would definitely be there for 7 p.m. so we agreed that dinner would be at 7 p.m. on the 11th March followed by my Anointing.

Chapter 43– I meet My Anaesthetist

As I am the Hon. Treasurer of the Parkinson UK - Eastbourne Branch the year-end is always a busy time as I have to present the financial statements to the Committee on the first Monday in January. Then I have to collate them in a different format for HQ and then put them in a simple form for my disabled brothers and sisters as well as their Spouses/Partners/Carers. Then I have to write "My Speech". This year I don't think I am going to make the AGM on 24th March. It just depends how quickly I get out of hospital and how quickly they get me walking again.

Before going on our little jaunt up north I had had the Committee Meeting when I disclosed the true state of the finances. I also had sent a draft copy of the year-end accounts to HQ and told them I did not expect any changes at the AGM which was going to be held on 24th March which was after the deadline of the end of February. There was nothing I could do about this so that was that.

I had also done the figures for the AGM in simple layman's terms and had written my speech. So I was all prepared ….

But the 24th March was only 12 days after my operation date so I knew that I may not be there and young Barry Weise, in his first year as my deputy,

147

would be slung in the deep end, without a paddle to support him. A baptism of fire so to speak but, I am sure, that he will cope admirably. But unbeknown to any of us the Chinese were talking about a killer virus and that they had closed down Wuhan city. Little did we know how much this would affect peoples' way of life all around the globe.

With the 26th February being only just around the corner once again Mick arranged patient transport for a two-hour pre-op assessment at the NHIM. Patient transport arrived promptly at 10.30 and it was the first taxi driver we had had for this journey. I had a quiet word with him about our previous adventure whilst Mick was locking up the house. (Holly Dog had already been delivered to my Mum for her day away).

Anyway, we set off and at first the driver was very careful but when we turned off the A22 and headed for Tunbridge Wells the demon driver popped out again. I had been quietly dozing in the back but on turning off the A22 he hit every cats eye, pothole and bump in the road. This lasted until we arrived in Tunbridge Wells when Mick asked him to stop, jumped out rapidly and was sick amongst some trees. When he got back in he said he did not think he was going to make it to the hospital. The driver asked him why he came along as I was the patient. To which I replied "The NHNN have told me that I cannot come without another person accompanying me. So he had no choice." I passed Mick a plastic bag, just in case and off we went again. Fortunately, we hit the M25 fairly soon after and I fell asleep. Mick had also nodded off and fortunately he stayed asleep nearly all the rest of the way there.

We arrived about half an hour early and I said to Mick we will go and let them know we are here just in case we are seen early. We had been sitting in reception for about three minutes when we were collected by Caleb, a very nice male nurse practitioner, who proceeded to go through my medications and ask me various questions. He then took me through the decompression surgery and told me that this involved the removal of certain parts of my L4 vertebra, i.e. The knob that you feel at the back and the arms that hold it on to the rest of the vertebra this means that the pinching would disappear and therefore the pain in both of my legs would go away. I did ask him whether the remaining half of the vertebra could float away from my spine but was assured that this could not happen as there were other things keeping it in place.

He then gave me a bag of goodies which was basically a Hibiscrub with which I had to wash myself and my hair in the shower for the five days prior to surgery and some stuff to put up my nose three times a day. These combined to kill off the bacteria crawling around on my skin so there was even less chance of infection. He then took a couple of swabs looking for the MRSA bug as people can carry it but not actually get sick themselves. He then took me through all the answers, and he stopped when it flashed that I was anaemic. He asked me if I had said I was. To which I replied, "I was never asked the question." So he removed that particular statement. After he had given me various forms for blood tests together with a map of the hospital he went to check if the anaesthetist was ready to see me and he came back to say she would be ready shortly. So we were escorted back to the waiting area when a few minutes later another young doctor came to fetch us and introduced herself as my anaesthetist.

She went through my forms writing on them the exact dates when I had to stop taking my Evening Primrose Oil which was a week before, the Methotrexate not to take the Wednesday before the operation and no Alendronic Acid on the day of the operation. My blood thinners, Pradaxa, I should stop taking three days beforehand, but this might change if the blood tests showed any problems with my kidneys. But if this was the case, they would speak with me over the phone on Friday. I informed her that as I was a sicky person so would they put something in the anaesthetic so that I wasn't sick after the operation as I did not fancy retching with a sore back. She told me not to worry as they did that as a matter of course at the NHNN and therefore at the NHIM as well. So we left her and went to do the blood tests. We traced our steps outside and round the back to the Basil Samuel Outpatient

The Art of Falling Gracefully

Department where I usually saw Professor Tom about my Parkinson's. After five minutes, my number came up and they showed me where to go. The nurse there was yet another kind person and must have been very good at her job because I never felt a thing and neither was my arm all battered and bruised like it normally is when I have a blood test done. After taking 8 phials of blood and with the bleeding under control we left.

We called the driver who was there waiting for us when we re-emerged into the weak sunlight and we were off home. Mick and I both ate a roll very slowly and followed it with an apple as, with something in our stomachs, I thought that the journey would be easier. I fell asleep once we were out of London and dozed all the way until we were nearly home.

Once home we had our usual cup of tea and I rang Mum firstly to check on Holly Dog and then to tell her that yes, they were going to do the operation. Mick left to get Holly Dog back. The next day Mick was out most of it, so I had a bit of a lazy day but the post on Friday bought a bit of a shock. It appeared that I was mildly anaemic with a blood count of 117. The letter went on to say that the NHNN looked for a count of 130. They had written to my GP to apprise her of the situation, so I had to make an urgent appointment with her to get some iron tablets.

As my GP only works Monday to Wednesday, I waited

for Monday morning and then tried to get an appointment to see her. "So sorry" the receptionist said and continued "she is fully booked today. I suggest you try tomorrow". I replied, "Tomorrow might be too late." I continued "I am due to have major back surgery in London at the NHIM, which is part of the NHNN, on Friday 13th March and blood tests have shown that I am anaemic so I have to speak with my GP today and obtain a prescription or they may not operate. Could you possibly ask her to ring me at home either before 1 o'clock or after 3 o'clock as I am due at the hospital for hydrotherapy between those times." So the receptionist left a message.

My GP rang me at 12.20 and said she had already done a prescription for me and dispatched it to Kamsons Pharmacy. She asked me how I was and to let her know how the operation went when I was back home. I agreed to keep her informed. After hydrotherapy Mick drove me to the pharmacy where I picked up one month's supply of iron pills and found out I had to take three every day and have a blood test after three months.

I just hope they work so my operation is not postponed......

The Art of Falling Gracefully

Chapter 44 - Indoor Motorised Transportation Arrives

You will, my readers, remember that after the last major fall when I landed in A&E I agreed with my physiotherapist, Debbie, that I would acquire a powered wheelchair for use at home and I had seriously been thinking about it. With my operation two weeks away, I suggested to Mick that now was the time for me to go and get one as if I fell on my back afterwards I could possibly do myself a real mischief. He agreed so off we went to Hilliers Garden Centre in Hailsham which is so much more than just a place to get stuff for the garden. It's a mini village under one roof selling some special food items to shoes and clothing to bedlinen and items for the disabled such as myself.

We sat down, with Holly Dog in tow, in front of a very nice young man and I explained that I wanted a powered wheelchair that would not just go forward and backwards but up and down as well. He said that he had just the thing and guided me to a wheelchair and sat me in it. He turned it on and explained the controls. He told me to give it a go so off I went. Boy, but that control stick was very fierce, and I knew I would bash not bump into skirting boards, doors and wreck my new kitchen. He then sat me in something else and said that this had a much better gear stick and it was. I loved it. No bumping into skirting boards etc. with this one. Shame it did not go up and down. So we left.

Two days later we went to Orange Badge Mobility in Lewes and I sat down in a powered chair which rose up 12 inches. The sales assistant, who was extremely knowledgeable asked me to try the joystick so I did and, wonder upon wonders, it was even more user friendly than the one I had tried at the "garden centre" where I had also been told that there was nothing else on the market except what they sold. I asked the price and was told that each chair was individually made for that person and delivery was about 6 weeks. I told him that I was going into hospital in a week for major back surgery.

He thought that apart from the seat this wheelchair could have been made for me so off he went to see if they could sell me the chair, I was sitting in. I practiced going round the showroom and did not bump into anything. He came back after a while saying that they had printed out the price list and he handed the list suitably marked up to show the cost of the chair. As various people had put their bottoms onto the seat, they would knock £500 off the price. Mick said did they know about the discount arrangement many of the shops in Lewes had with the Lewes F.C. No said our sales guy. So Mick then explained that he was a part owner of Lewes F.C. (I didn't hear him say his investment was a mere £30) and as such he was entitled to various discounts from various shops and were they a member of this scheme?

He tried bless him but at the same time he passed over a Bank Card and I had another opportunity to try going through some narrow doorways which I knew could be a struggle when walking due to my predilection for freezing. Do you know I did not bump into anything although I was a bit hesitant? Anyway, with a 50% deposit paid, I took my chair back to its friends and this time I did not hesitate at all.

Thursday morning arrived and the phone rang to arrange delivery the following week and it was agreed that it would come between 9 and 11 o'clock Tuesday morning. I have every confidence that it will be fine. I just wonder if he remembers to put a cable clip for my walker with the package as he promised......!

Chapter 45 – The Anointing of the Sick (previously known as The Last Rites)

The easiest meal to cook for Fr. Raglan, who is our parish priest (remember that he organised the choir to pay for the hall on a donation basis) was a roast dinner because I had made them so often I just put it in the oven and go and sit down. Fr. Raglan phoned me at 6 p.m. to say he was stuck in traffic and could he still come for dinner. To which I replied "Of course. I will delay putting the vegetables on till you arrive."

I thought to myself we have been here before when I was 16 years old. Let me explain. At 16 we moved into a four-bedroom bungalow A short time later we asked the parish priest to come and bless the house and he could have his tea with us as well. He duly arrived and we all sat down and ate. My Dad stood up and said we will just clear the things away and then you can do the Blessing of the House.

Well I have never seen a priest more put out as he had to admit that he had forgotten to bring the items with him to bless the house. My brothers and I thought it was too funny especially since he said he would do it next time he came. Mum whispered to me that there was not going to be a next time.

As it happened Fr Raglan made good time and was with us just after 6.30 p.m. We sat down immediately to some pate on toast whilst I cooked the veggies. Then we had the roast chicken followed by a raspberry and strawberry crumble. He said the flavours in the dinner were wonderful and then said, to my relief, "Where shall we sit to do the Anointing." We ushered him into the front room, and I sat down. He got out his prayer book and commended me to God and anointed my forehead and the palms of my hands. He left shortly after as he had been out most of the day and he had to see if anyone needed him urgently.

Now all I had to do was wait and hope that tomorrow being Thursday was the day before my operation and patient transport was ordered for 3.00 p.m. would arrive on time.

Chapter 46 – My First Surgery

For the first time when we booked patient transport, we hit a snag. Mick was told quite categorically by the lady at the end of the telephone that he could not come, and that the driver would take my suitcase to the ward and "hand me over" so to speak. I said to the lady that so long as the driver was going to do that then it was OK. For me, it was a relief not to have to listen to Mick throwing up.

Joe arrived on time at 3 p.m. We told him what had happened I asked him if he had been told about taking my suitcase up to the ward. No nothing had been said to him besides if he left his car he would be fined. We told him that patient transport had said that they did not allow escorts as often the cars took more than one patient. "Rubbish," he replied, "Taxis only take one patient." Joe asked Mick if he was coming with us which he answered "Yes" but we had to phone my Mum to send my brother Francis, who was staying with her to keep her calm whilst I had my operation, to come and get Holly Dog. Meanwhile we loaded up the car. Francis appeared before we had finished and with Mick having taken his Kwells and with his wallet in his pocket we left. The journey was a nightmare as we hit traffic all the way there but once we got on the M25 we could shift along and yes I fell asleep and yes Mick was sick with all the stopping and starting. It became painfully clear that I was not going to arrive for 6 p.m. so I phoned ahead and told the staff nurse. I was told not to worry but just to arrive safely. We were as it happened 45 minutes late.!!!!

Mick took me to Victor Horsely Ward which was going to be my home for the next four nights. Bay 4 had six beds in it and all were temporarily occupied. I was in bed 6. Settling in proved to be a trifle difficult as there was no cupboard for me to put anything in. The following morning the doctors came round to say that the operating theatres might be closing and in which case we would be sent home.

That thought was just unthinkable. I was supposed to be the first one down but was told it would be about 10.30 or so. Well 10.30 came and went and so did 12.30. At about 2 p.m. they came and got my friend in bed 1. Half an hour later a porter appeared at the bottom of my bed and said, "Veronika Lees?"
"Yes" said I.
"It's your turn" he said, and I was taken away.

We arrived outside the theatre to be met by the registrar and a lady nurse who had pink hair. She showed me my consent form and asked if the tiny squiggle was mine. "Yes," I said, "I have Parkinson's and can no longer write legibly." The next thing I was told was that when I awoke, I would find I had odd cannula in and not to worry. They would put something in my wrist on my left hand to monitor my blood pressure. He then injected the anaesthetic and I knew no more............

I must have woken up properly a few hours later on the ward and I decided to take stock. My left hand had two cannulas in the back of it and a pressure bandage on the wrist which latterly sported a bruise three inches by two inches. I had a drain in my back which is not uncommon after any operation, but I also had two pipes sticking up my nose for oxygen. I slowly raised the bed head and looked around.........

The first thing I saw was the lady in bed 1 was being brought back on her bed and she was still very sleepy. One of the nurses came over to ask me how I was feeling to which I replied I was good, but I was hungry. So she went to see what she could find and came back with a repeat of yesterday's chicken casserole. I made swift work of it together with a cup of tea. I decided that before I closed my eyes for the night I would wander to the toilets very slowly so I removed the oxygen tube up my nose and grabbed the edge of the bed just in case I fell. I stood up. There was no pain. I picked up my stick and with drain-bag in hand went very slowly to the loo with a nurse keeping a watchful eye at me. I went in and closed the door and after doing what I had to, washed my hands. By this time, I was drenched in sweat and I staggered very slowly back to bed.

Morning came and after a very late breakfast at about 9.30 the doctors came on their rounds. They asked me if I had any pain to which I replied none. They checked my drain and saw that there was 150 ml of blood in it and decided it had to be less than 100ml for it to be taken away. Had I gotten up yet. Yes, I went for a walk to the toilet last night and there was no pain in my legs at all. I just had a minor niggle in my back." We will see you tomorrow" they said and then left.

Lunch came and went, and Mick arrived armed with various offerings including my orange juice and lemonade. All my friends know I hate the taste of drinking water by itself. I wanted to wash my hair and there was mention that there was some hot water in one of the showers so armed with a bottle of shampoo and conditioner and a towel we went to investigate.

The water ran cold but gradually warmed up just a tad. I decided to go for it. So holding the shower curtain round me Mick pointed the shower at my head and proceeded to wet not just my hair but also my face, my arms and my body. Fortunately, the temperature of the water was by then about moderate. I should mention at this point Mick has only once before done my hair for me and this was several months previously over the bath. I towel dried it once my afternoon's drowning was at an end. Returning to my bed I got Mick to help me to pack up a few things for him to take home. He then left and said he would be back on

The Art of Falling Gracefully

Monday. I spent a quiet Sunday pottering around getting my strength back. My drain was removed as there was less than 50ml extra in the bag. I was glad to see the back of that extra handbag; you see twice I set off without it and got hauled back on the stitch that kept my drain in my back.

Monday came and the doctors came round and said I could go home. I told them I needed patient transport and they asked the nurse to arrange it. I said that Mick was coming up so later on would be fine. I went and washed and dressed for the first time and started my packing. My lunch appeared and afterwards I resumed my packing. Mick appeared at about two o'clock in time to shut my suitcase and to receive my discharge letter. I waited for the pharmacist to come so that I could ask about the recommencement of my medication that was stopped.

Meanwhile a message came that my transport was waiting downstairs, so arranging to speak with the pharmacist the next day, we left.

Pedro was waiting for us when we got outside. As usual Mick got in the front and I climbed slowly in the back. Pedro told us that he had disinfected his car for us so we could not catch the coronavirus that was rapidly spreading around the globe. We warned Pedro that motto of the day was "no potholes please". Off we went. Pedro was an entertainment in itself, and it wasn't long before we were bowling down the M25 home. The traffic was extraordinarily light. We were home just after 6.30. As usual we had a cup of tea and Mick took all my stuff upstairs and then went to get Holly Dog.

After being away for several nights Holly Dog ran amok when she saw me sitting in my usual chair and danced back and forth for a good five minutes before Mick was able to pick her up and put her into my lap for a cuddle.

It was, it has to be said, lovely to be pain free and home again.

Chapter 47 – Self-Isolation

I had to be careful not to fall down and was told by the doctors at the hospital to rest. I did just that. Mick had done some shopping prior to my return so food was not a problem. He stayed with me just in case I had to get up. I think I spent about three days at home in my nightie and dressing gown as I was too tired to dress. I also caught up with the coronavirus outbreak in China and was quite shocked to see how many people were infected across Europe. Just how did it spread so quickly? It became clear on the news that the coronavirus was the sole topic together with how the NHS was coping. No Brexit news at all nor was there anything on the trade agreement with Europe.

By the time I had been home for nearly a week the country was in lockdown. We were all asked to stay at home and only go out for food, medicine, a walk or to look after a vulnerable person. The first Sunday I was at home after my operation, people all flocked to the coast and to National Trust places as the weather was so warm so Boris Johnson, the Prime Minister, went on TV to say he had asked people politely to stay home but now he was ordering everyone who could to do so. The police would question anyone on the streets and issue instant fines where they deemed it necessary. By the time we had been self-isolating for two weeks the UK had 19,567 confirmed cases with 140 people recovered and 1,228 deaths in hospitals.

The Art of Falling Gracefully

By the middle of May there were approximately 34,000 dead.

A week after I was home, I had to have my stitches out so, having booked a nurse at our GP's for 1.15 p.m. we climbed into the car and dashed to Green Street. There was no one about so I got out the car and walked as quickly as I could to the surgery. Getting into the surgery was a feat in itself as I was met with a locked door. On ringing the bell, I was asked who I was and what did I want. I told them my name and date of birth and then said I booked an appointment last week to have my stitches out. Have you got a fever or a cough the voice asked, which I answered 'no'. Push the door I was told and in I went.

The nurse whipped my stitches out very carefully, but the wound still opened just a little. She told me I could shower but not to lie in a bath for a week. So I left after thanking her as I had not felt a thing when she took them out.

With nobody in the Co-op or indeed in the greengrocer Mick did some additional shopping and we dashed home again. Our daughter did some shopping during the week for bread, milk and toilet paper, which was virtually impossible to get due to the madness of the British people who panicked and stripped the shelves of everything in the supermarkets and then threw it out a week later when they discovered they could not eat it all.

In our third week of isolation, life had settled down to a regular pattern. Using a tool called "Zoom" we have half an hour of singing at 10.30 a.m. on Mondays, Wednesdays and Thursdays and at 9.55 a.m. on Tuesdays. The first time we did this we could not stop laughing as we saw, for the first time, the faces which the choir pulled when they were singing as the more usual thing is for the choir to sit in rows with the ladies on the right and the gentlemen on the left.

We are also keeping in touch with all the Parkinson people we know as each Committee Member has taken on board half a dozen people or so and again has weekly meetings via Zoom. These meetings are on a Tuesday which is our regular day when the Eastbourne Parkinson's Branch would have met. They are preceded on a Monday afternoon with a half hour Committee Meeting when our Chairperson, Veronica Stoner, tells us any news that she thinks we should disseminate down to our members. We have also included those who only come to choir, or just to hydrotherapy and those who go to the Saturday gym sessions. Our aim is to keep everyone going with something to look forward to. Our first meeting included a quiz which was devised by Mick. He has said he will continue to provide such quizzes every week for everyone to try. But we hope in due time to get recordings from the visiting speakers which we had booked but obviously had to cancel.

We don't know how long we will be in lockdown. The "Powers that be" are now telling people to return to work but to wear face masks and observe social distancing and to travel to work on foot, or by bicycle or in one's car thus avoiding public transport. The first day back the roads were in gridlock as so many people drove to work in their cars. I just pray that all my family and all my friends make it through, and we will meet up again.

But one thing I do know we have missed several opportunities for fundraising. We will probably have to revisit the budget when eventually we can do so because, I suspect, with no fund raising done this financial year and no trips undertaken we may be in a position to be passing funds onto Parkinson's UK for research into finding a cure for Parkinson's. I also have discovered that the cost of running HQ, even with as many staff as possible furloughed, is £95,000 a week. Whilst they have raised £300,000, we will probably have to part with some of our cherished reserves which we have accumulated under my tenure as Treasurer. I have discussed this with the Committee, and they all agreed with me that we could afford to hand over £5,000, particularly as we have no idea when hydrotherapy will recommence.

I was supposed to be going for my post op check-up

on 30th April using patient transport, but Dr Akram's secretary phoned to postpone it until July. This time I have arranged to go on 10th July which is when I have my next meeting with Professor Tom to discuss my second surgery. I had hoped that he would then schedule the next operation of planting the gizmo in my back to take away the residual pain from Parkinson's and, with a bit of luck, will help my walking.

Further on 28th April I received a letter on the hospital portal My Care that I must remain in purdah for a further three months as the Methotrexate and the Hydroxychloroquine that I take for my chronic inflammatory arthritis has contravened my immune system, which makes it more likely that I can fall ill with the coronavirus and be in intensive care if I should come into contact with it

The coronavirus pandemic has made life very difficult and I can see myself having to wait until 2021 before the second surgery takes place. One thing I do know is that once the swelling went down my leg tremors resumed even worse than before (well it was 16 months ago that I fell and damaged my spine) and my hands have started to tremor as well, particularly when I hold something. As I am on maximum medication this may mean that the DBS could be back on the cards as well.

The Art of Falling Gracefully

We will all have to wait and see.......

Our previous Chairperson, Liz Ovenden, telephoned the morning of 3rd April, to tell us that her husband of 45 years had died that morning in hospital from a chest infection. He had also tested positive for coronavirus. Trevor was a lovely man who had suffered with Parkinson's for well over 20 years. May he rest in peace.

Veronika 19th May 2020

APPENDICES

Appendix 1

My Medication Prior to the First Surgery

5 .00 a.m.   Alendronic Acid 70 mg sit upright in
               bed and swallow with a glass of water.
               Remain upright for at least half
               an hour. Friday morning only...
               (to protect me from breaking my
               bones).

6,00 a.m.   One 25/100 mg Sinemet Plus.
               One 10 mg Cetirizine (antihistamine).
               One 200 mg Ferrous Sulphate
               (anaemia), and
               One 10 mg Buscopan (Wednesday's
               only to mop up excess saliva when
               singing).

8.00 a.m.   One 25/100 mg Sinemet Plus.
               5 ml of Amantadine Syrup.
               One 150 mg Pradaxa (blood thinners).
               One 200 mg Hydroxychloroquine
               (chronic inflammatory arthritis).
               300 mg of Gabapentin (nerve pain
               from spondylolisthesis), and
               One 10 mg Buscopan (Wednesday's
               only)

10.00 a.m.	One 25/100 mg Sinemet Plus, and One 10 mg Buscopan (Wednesday Only.
Noon	One 25/100 mg Sinemet Plus. 5 ml of Amantadine Syrup. One 200 mg Ferrous Sulphate (anaemia) 300 mg of Gabapentin. 20 mg Methotrexate (8*2.5mg) (Wednesday only for my chronic inflammatory arthritis), and 5 mg Folic Acid (Saturday only).
2.00 p.m.	One 25/100 mg Sinemet Plus.
4.00 p.m.	One 25/100 mg Sinemet Plus, and 1000 mg Evening Primrose Oil.
6.00 p.m.	One 25/100 mg Sinemet Plus One 200 mg Ferrous Sulphate (anaemia).
8.00 p.m.	One 25/100 mg Sinemet Plus: One 150mg Pradaxa, and 600 mg Gabapentin.
10.00 p.m.	Two Half Sinemet CR, and Calcium and Magnesium tablet.

The Art of Falling Gracefully

Also, for the nerve pain can have up to three times 5ml of Oramorphine together with Paracetamol and Ibuprofen.

I also have osteoarthritis in my feet and in my hips for which I have been prescribed Voltarol Emulgel Diclofenac which I can use up to three times a day, and Carbomer which is a liquid gel I use for dry eyes.

Appendix 11

My Medication After the First Surgery

5 .00 a.m.   Alendronic Acid 70 mg sit upright in bed and swallow with a glass of water. Remain upright for at least half an hour. Friday morning only...
(to protect me from breaking my bones).

6,00 a.m.   One 25/100 mg Sinemet Plus.
One 10 mg Cetirizine (antihistamine).
One 200 mg Ferrous Sulphate (anaemia), and
One 10 mg Buscopan (Wednesday's only to mop up excess saliva when singing).

8.00 am.   One 25/100 mg Sinemet plus.
5 ml of Amantadine Syrup

One 150 mg Pradaxa (blood thinners).
One 200mg Hydroxychloroquine (chronic inflammatory arthritis), and
One 10 mg Buscopan (Wednesday's only).

The Art of Falling Gracefully

10.00 a.m.   One 25/100 mg Sinemet Plus, and
                 One 10 mg Buscopan (Wednesday's
                 only).

Noon   One 25/100 mg Sinemet Plus.
                 5 ml of Amantadine Syrup
                 One 200 mg Ferrous Sulphate
                 (anaemia)
                 20 mg Methotrexate (8*2.5mg)
                 (Wednesday only for my chronic
                 inflammatory arthritis)
                 5 mg Folic Acid (Saturday only to
                 counter any side effects of the
                 Methotrexate).

2.00 p.m.   One 25/100 mg Sinemet Plus.

4.00 p.m.   One 25/100 mg Sinemet Plus, and
                 1000 mg Evening Primrose Oil,

6.00 p.m.   One 25/100 mg Sinemet Plus, and
                 One 200 mg Ferrous Sulphate

(anaemia).

8.00 p.m.   One 25/100 mg Sinemet Plus, and
                 One 150 mg Pradaxa.

10.00 p.m.   Two Half Sinemet CR, and
                 Calcium and Magnesium tablet.

The Ferrous Sulphate is a temporary medication and it was discovered at the pre-operation blood tests that I had anaemia.

I also have Voltarol Emulgel Diclofenac for my osteoarthritis and Carbomer liquid gel for dry eyes.

Notes

The Art of Falling Gracefully

Printed in Poland
by Amazon Fulfillment
Poland Sp. z o.o., Wrocław

62634778R00101